First published in the United States of America in 2020
by Henselstone Verlag LLC

First Edition

Every effort has been made to locate and contact
all holders of copyright to material reproduced in this book.
For information about permission to reproduce selections from this book, write to
Henselstone Verlag LLC, P.O. Box 201, Amissville, VA 20106.

Library of Congress Control Number 2020938093

Keyword Data
von Feilitzsch, Heribert, 1965-

The Negotiator's Toolbox: Winning Strategies for Corporate Buyers and
Small Businesses / Heribert von Feilitzsch.
p. cm
Includes biographical references.

ISBN 978-1-7349324-0-9 (paperback), 978-1-7349324-1-6 (e-book),
978-7349324-2-3 (audio book)

Negotiation
Negotiation in Business
Business – Negotiation - Purchasing
Negotiation in Business – Case Studies
Self-help Techniques – Negotiation
Self-help Techniques – Business
von Feilitzsch, Heribert. Title.

www.negotiatorstoolbox.com

Printed in the United States of America

THE NEGOTIATOR'S TOOLBOX

Winning Strategies for Corporate Buyers
and Small Businesses

Praise for

The Negotiator's Toolbox

The Negotiator's Toolbox is a must-have addition to the library of anyone wishing to better understand the key elements involved in having a successful negotiation. Von Feilitzsch provides great insights into understanding yourself, your team, and the entities you are negotiating with. He helps focus on proper preparation before the negotiation session, and identifies the ways in which a negotiator can seek to better understand the motivation and objectives of the other parties involved. His concise explanation of relationship building and other key concepts is insightful. In addition, his use of meaningful anecdotes to illustrate the key points make the lessons easy to understand and apply. I highly recommend this book to all who wish to be more successful in sales, client relationships, and all manner of business interactions.

Gary W. Noesner
Chief, FBI Crisis Negotiation Unit (retired)
Author of *Stalling for Time: My Life as an FBI Hostage Negotiator*

For the love of my life

Contents

List of Illustrations

Credit for all portrait and figure photography:
Mina von Feilitzsch Photography

Preface

How many negotiations do you conduct each day?

This is one of the questions I like to pose to the audience in my speeches and seminars. Ten? Fifty? Eighty?

The likely answer is that on average you are negotiating more than one hundred times each day!

How many of these instances do you consciously recognize as negotiations? How many do you prepare? Have defined goals? And a strategy?

For most of these normal, everyday negotiations you don't need to prepare or even spend much thought on preparation. But for important negotiations related to your personal and professional life, you need to prepare well to extract the optimal result.

Heribert von Feilitzsch wrote this book in order to help fix this issue for negotiators in the future. He explains how he successfully coaches clients in their toughest negotiations as a professional negotiator for Frieder Gamm Group. Through seminars and individual coaching sessions, our customers learn how to prepare professionally, and effectively execute challenging negotiations for a successful conclusion.

Let him show you how to integrate psychology, behavioral science, and communication theory into easy to use tools to develop strategies and tactics, as well as to uncover manipulation in negotiations.

Von Feilitzsch is one of the best negotiators with whom I've ever had the pleasure to work. He explains how you, too, can become one of the best.

Frieder Gamm
Frieder Gamm Group GmbH, Stuttgart
Frieder Gamm Group USA LLC, Winston-Salem, NC

Introduction

"I t's time to die!" a well-known book on negotiation begins, and tension builds from there.[1] I am fascinated by accounts of former hostage negotiators. The authors, high-powered stars of our federal law enforcement, appear larger than life, and the stakes of the scenarios they describe could not be higher. In most cases, the perpetrators are suicidal, desperate, or mentally ill. Leverage is virtually non-existent. Yet, in many cases these negotiators still manage to eke out a release of the hostages and a peaceful outcome. How much more exciting could negotiations be?

The question is whether these hostage negotiation techniques are transferable to a business environment. Many of the participants in my negotiation training seminars have been to one or more of former FBI negotiator seminars, and most return in awe of the stories, but with few practical tools to apply in their daily business. After all, many of us are not psychologists, nor do we often, if ever, find ourselves in life-or-death situations. We need simple, down-to-earth, easy-to-use tools explained with practical examples that relate directly to our daily lives in business. This is my goal for this book. I've adapted some of the hostage negotiators' main tools for our purpose of

---

[1] Noesner, Gary, *Stalling for Time: My Life as an FBI Hostage Negotiator* (New York: Random House, 2010), chapter 1 title.

negotiating in a business environment. I particularly liked the hostage negotiators' use of cooperative strategies rather than pressure strategies. I also endorse separating the role of negotiators from final decision makers. I subscribe to psychologically enhanced questioning techniques, and communicating with precision. I also added lots of additional techniques in the book as a toolkit.

I differ from the hostage negotiators with respect to the environment in which I operate. Life-threatening stakes imply stress and pressure, a fear of catastrophic failure. Although I did experience existential fears when I started out in business, experienced businesspeople I respected firmly guided me in reframing my perspective. I wanted to succeed at all costs at the start of my career, never make a mistake, and climb the corporate ladder—no matter the trail of collateral damage and ruined relationships I left in my wake.

One day I discussed a business plan for a company I wanted to start with my uncle, a World War II veteran. I told him about my existential fear of failure: that I would lose my house, my wife, my kids, my savings—basically life as I knew it if my plan did not work. Instead of sympathy, my uncle laughed. Having come out of the Russian theater of war, having spent years in a labor camp, and having seen his comrades blown apart right next to him, he had no fear. He had been in truly life-threatening situations. Suddenly, a light bulb went on in my head. I realized why his generation, that also includes my father-in-law who served on the opposite side as a frontline munitions-bearer, built the post-war world with such success. It was a generation that functioned with motivators other than fear. They had to rebuild an utterly destroyed landscape—in the case of Germany literally starting from scratch. They had to use whatever was available. Get it done. Find a way. Solve the problem. Make a deal. Compromise.

I realized then that in my world of global trade, industry, and small business, there was no place for existential fears. A failed negotiation hardly costs lives in business. In the worst case, you lose your next bonus or promotion. Mistakes are there to learn from, and hopefully not to repeat them. My uncle and father-in-law taught me that negotiating should be fun. Since then, my feeling of dread before a negotiation has vanished. The challenge of figuring out how to get into my counterpart's head, how to elicit crucial information, and what I can do to come to an agreement excites me. For me, negotiation has become a game, with rules (yes, ethics count!), often with high stakes, lots of possible outcomes, and many layers of technique and skill. Negotiating is at the same time complicated, challenging—certainly never boring—and creative. If you master the art of negotiation, then you've become a master at this game. Negotiating a good agreement, with everyone getting something out of it, and relationships staying intact for the next round, now that is fun!

Which negotiations have been the most interesting in my experience? Those that resonate with my empathy for the hostage negotiators. I thrive in situations where there is a lot at stake, and the odds of coming to a good agreement are low. That has been my job for many years. Facing a monopolist, the only source for what I needed to buy; having no apparent leverage; maybe even dealing with a counterpart who was threatening, aggressive, and with whom it was hard to get along. Those are the negotiations I used to loathe and now love to master. Weakness is strength. 'No' is a word with which I can work. I have fun negotiating. I celebrate when I succeed, and I study my mistakes when I don't. This book explains all the basic negotiation tools you'll need to win tough negotiations. It introduces innovative psychological concepts, giving you an advantage in your industry or your business.

I designed this book for anyone who negotiates, something we do all the time starting with who lets the dog out in the morning. But the professional negotiations are the ones that will energize our careers—and that can also sink them. During my years as a coach and trainer, I specialized on the buying side of the negotiation equation. The sales side of the equation has lots of advantages and already offers a wealth of resources. You will discover in this book that salespeople often are better equipped to succeed at negotiations based upon a set of common personality traits. They are naturally extroverted, communicate easily, ask good questions, can dial back their egos, and often spend their entire careers successfully negotiating from a position of weakness.

Buyers live in a different world, and experience a different landscape. Their personality traits tend to differ greatly from those of salespeople. They also receive little professional training. Most buyers learn on the job, while most salespeople take advantage of thorough training. There was not even a course of study for buyers until a few years ago. They usually came from the internal world of organizations, production or engineering departments, and only rarely switched sides from sales. The same is true for small business owners, where 'CEO' often means Chief-Everything-Officer. Most smaller companies do not even have a dedicated Purchasing Department. They may likely have someone in the back office who learned by doing.

The idea for this book formed during my years working in the textile and automotive industries in industrial engineering, sales, and market development. The period during which I ran a joint venture in the automotive industry between two fierce competitors taught me especially valuable lessons. I learned to be exceptionally sensitive to reading different people's motivations and to be extremely creative in my strategies and tactics working with them.

I decided to build my own company after ten years as a corporate soldier, and as many moves with my family. In nearly twenty years as the Chief-Everything-Officer of this small but successful company with little purchasing power, I honed my negotiation skills on a daily basis. I stayed connected with my automotive customers at the same time. I started a parallel career fifteen years ago as a negotiation trainer, coach, and ghost negotiator for large automotive original equipment manufacturers (OEMs). Having worked around the globe as a market developer and corporate executive, I saw a need for this new role by virtue of my unique cultural perspective as a bilingual German native living and working in the American South.

The most challenging, but also the most fascinating job I do, is ghost negotiations. I help companies prepare important negotiations, coach the negotiators, and, in some cases, conduct the negotiation under an assumed role. Clients have paid generously over the years to fix negotiations that had failed in an earlier go-around. I am not complaining. The work is rewarding. In fact, I love the challenge of negotiating myself out of a hole. But, why dig a hole in the first place? What are the pitfalls of steering a negotiation into failure and how to avoid them? You will find practical guidelines on how to prepare and execute negotiations in this book.

My most common observation over the years of training buyers in the automotive, energy generation, construction, and heavy equipment industries is this: As a buyer you are fairly safe using pressure in a corporate environment that glorifies just that. However, the business model, especially in the automotive industry (but everywhere else, too), has fundamentally shifted. Expertise for developing products moved from the in-house engineering departments to the suppliers. Parts that used to be assembled in-house are now integrated into fully assembled, plug-in systems. Suppliers carry the largest share of the development responsibility. Consequently, they are now also the ones with the leverage from their knowledge base and control over the specification.

Eventually, these suppliers become the sole sources of the parts, the Monopolists. In short, power has shifted away from the OEMs to the supply base. Yet, our negotiation culture remains stuck in 'P'—not 'partnership', but 'pressure'. And the results show it. In the past two decades, OEMs have not been successful in getting the best deal from suppliers. Why would suppliers give you the lowest offer, if they are forced to provide inflated and unrealistic "productivity" discounts over the next three to five years? They simply add it to the front end of their pricing and release it slowly over the contract period.

I have some favorite customers, appendages of large OEMs that don't quite fit the mold, such as Bentley Motors in Crewe, UK; Porsche during the years when the car maker was a small player in the industry; Daimler Bus Company in Toronto, Canada; and several divisions of Siemens. What do they have in common? Low bargaining power. Can they be successful? You judge! When Porsche united with VW, the big brother in Wolfsburg was shocked to see the purchase prices the thrifty Swabians had achieved. In some cases, parts were even cheaper for them than for VW at a much lower volume. How did the buyers at Porsche do it? I will explain.

Despite management nurturing pressure-based corporate cultures, I can help you get better results. Shouldn't your standard be to win negotiations consistently? I want to assemble for you a well-stocked toolbox that includes strategic, tactical, psychological, and behavioral tools. These are not only your hammers, wrenches, and screw drivers, but also your laser levels, humidity detectors, pressure gauges, as well as safety gloves and protective equipment that will help you in any situation of low bargaining power. And I will assemble these in such a way that you can immediately apply what you have learned. *The Negotiator's Toolbox* is divided into four main parts: Preparing the starting position, setting goals and strategies, executing the negotiation, and practice using the tools with real case studies.

Of course, success hinges upon practice—lots of it—which is up to you. Imagine your counterparts, the tough monopolists who seem to hold all the power, but only have one tool to use: Pressure. Let's get busy and put lots of new tools into our toolboxes and have some fun!

PART 1:
Preparing the Starting Position – Where am I?

Preparing for a negotiation takes a lot of work. I know, I know, you all are busy, and you may be short on time. Fine. Then concentrate on the negotiations where there is a lot at stake! I guarantee you that hiring someone like me to help fix a negotiation that has gone off the rails costs more and takes away more of your valuable time than if you had prepared better.

Step One in any negotiation is the starting position. I will show you what is important to know to develop goals and strategies. Yes, setting goals, developing strategies and planning tactics follow the preparation of the starting position, not the other way around. As a guideline, you should spend about 70% of your preparation time on the starting position.

CHAPTER 1: Who has the Power?

Power in a negotiation derives from many backgrounds: The existence of alternate suppliers, leverage based on quality problems, the prospect of important new future projects, and many others. Here's a short story that illustrates how a former boss of mine, who was typically an excellent negotiator, underestimated the power of his opponent.

I lived near Washington DC at the time, and my boss in France. We were headed to an important meeting on the West Coast. We decided that my boss, Jean-Louis, and I would meet at Dulles International Airport in Washington DC and that we would continue together to San Francisco from there. Jean-Louis's flight had been a nightmare. The plane had departed late. The business class seat had a broken audio system and, to top things off, a loud, screaming toddler had rattled the seatback for the entire eight-hour flight. My boss's stress level was already in the red zone. Not a good way to start a negotiation.

We met up and proceeded to the ticket counter for a well-known but unnamed carrier. Jean-Louis abhorred this airline because he found the service horrible, the personnel rude, and the equipment old. But there we were. Jean-Louis casually flipped his gold status frequent-flyer card on the counter with our passports. The agent behind the counter did not react. He was on his cell phone, obviously discussing something important with his girlfriend. We waited. We waited some more. I could tell that Jean-Louis was getting aggravated. His fingers drummed on the counter. Finally, he leaned over it.

"Excuse me!" he exclaimed.

The service representative flipped his cell phone closed (yes, it was that long ago), but his look told me that he did not appreciate the interruption. He checked us in. We had booked first class tickets. Jean-Louis looked at the attendant when he saw his seat assignment.

"I specifically requested a first-row seat!"

"I am sorry, Sir, that is already booked." The service representative looked annoyed.

"Do you know, how much I fly?" Jean-Louis gasped, his face turning into an explosive, deep red. I intervened.

"Just sit down over there." I grabbed him by the elbow. "I got this."

I went back to the counter. I tried for a disarming smile and a dismissive gesture, and started my campaign to get Jean-Louis the seat he wanted. I apologized for my boss. I explained that he had had a horrible flight and that he was really exhausted. I also mentioned how much I liked this airline and that it once even carried my dog on a seat in business class for free. Great service, I added. This was actually a true story. One minute later, I had scored Seat 1A for him.

That done, we went on to the security check. A TSA security officer checked our boarding passes. He motioned to Jean-Louis. "You! Come with me," he said.

Jean-Luis went through an enhanced security check, something that anywhere else in the world is called a strip search. It took twenty minutes of undressing, having all the hand luggage emptied, the laptop scrutinized, and his shoes scanned for bomb-making material residue several times before he emerged on the other side. He was fuming. What had happened? The kid behind the counter had printed "SSSS" on Jean-Louis's boarding pass, a sign for the TSA agents to consider my boss a high security risk. Nice! Who, in this case had the power? The guy with the gold level frequent-flyer card and the first-class ticket, or the customer service agent with access to a keyboard? You guessed right! Never underestimate where the power lies.

CHAPTER 2: Benchmarks and Data

This chapter is purposefully brief for the corporate buyers and managers among us. You are working in professional environments and already know how to work within the systems you have.

However, these systems are usually not available to professionals working in small businesses. You have to jump through different sets of hoops to get the data you need to prepare a negotiation. Think of ways to establish the regular collection of data as you are chasing it down in the checklist below. There is nothing wrong with using spreadsheets! I know from my own experience that much of this data is hidden in archived e-mails or not at all. Collect this data on a regular basis and update your files as new information floats across your desk.

Frequently, issues like quality defects might not even make it to your desk. I was shocked to find out in an exit interview of an employee that in my own company we had serious quality problems in the field. Why did I not know? My employees repaired and corrected these mistakes without documentation. The pervasive thought was that we expected them to make any necessary fixes in the field to shield our company from customer complaints. A noble thought to be sure, but their failure to report back all the facts resulted in our senior management assuming that supplier quality was good when it actually was not.

If you are working as a buyer (or have the purchasing function as part of your area of responsibility), consistently try to keep up with the standing of your suppliers within the market and their industry. Collect financial information to see if they are making larger than industry-average profits. If so, you can count on a competitor coming after them to gain market share, as well. Make sure you know when that occurs and who that particular competitor is. Either it becomes a potentially viable supplier for you, or you might realize big discounts in your current negotiation. Large companies consistently underestimate the information that we, as small businesses, can collect. That makes them lazy in their preparation of negotiations with you. Use that laziness to your advantage! It is worth the extra time spent on research.

Here are some of the pertinent questions you need to answer:

Benchmark and Data Checklist

✓ What is the **price history** of the part or service ?
  ☐ Has the supplier ever given a discount?
  ☐ If so, what was it?
  ☐ Did the supplier increase prices in the past?
  ☐ If so, under what circumstances?

✓ What is the **quality performance** of the supplier?
  ☐ Are there any known quality defects?
  ☐ Any pending claims?
  ☐ In the automotive industry, what is the ppm rate (parts per million defects)?

- ☐ Is the Logistics Department satisfied with the current supplier?
- ☐ Have there been delivery issues in the past?
- ☐ If so, were they solved?
- ☐ How?
- ☐ Is the manufacturing/production department satisfied with the supplier?
- ☐ If there were any issues, what were they?
- ☐ Have they been addressed?

✓ What is the **engagement** of the supplier?
- ☐ Is the product development/engineering department satisfied with the supplier?
- ☐ Are they responsive?
- ☐ Are they innovative?
- ☐ Do they have a future with the current product development group?
- ☐ If not, why?
- ☐ Did the supplier gain access to your new projects? Dropping a supplier for new projects may seriously weaken the bargaining position for current supplies.

✓ How does the supplier fare in its **industry**?
- ☐ Is it a leader or follower?
- ☐ Does that match what you are looking for?
- ☐ Who are the competitors?
- ☐ What are their strengths and weaknesses?
- ☐ Are any of them released by engineering, quality control, and accounting to supply you?

  If you are lacking a lot of this information, and you cannot find it online or within the organization, consider inviting the supplier to make a company presentation to you. Mandate that they specifically address the industry, their place in it, and their plans.

✓ What is the *financial situation* of the supplier?
- ☐ Is it a public or a private company?
  The answer to this question will be very important later in the book when we discuss strategy and tactics.
- ☐ What is its cash flow, revenue, cost chain?
- ☐ Does it have a history of financial woes or changing ownership?
- ☐ Where are the main products manufactured?
- ☐ Where are their main raw materials sourced?

     Get your financial department to provide credit history, Dun and Bradstreet reports, and any other available information. Many privately owned businesses are very careful about not sharing financial information. Talk to their competitors, visit their facilities, chat with their sales staff. Shaking the tree can allow a lot of fruitful information to fall down. We will discuss the loose lips of salespeople later in the book.

CHAPTER 3: Alternative Sources

O ne of the most critical questions you must ask yourself is if there is an alternative supplier. Can you buy the same product from someone else or, conversely, for the salespeople among us, can you sell the same product to someone else? Having an alternate source relaxes the negotiation quite a bit. You can set your goals higher. You also can use strategies and tactics that are more aggressive. Yet, in the many negotiations I have coached, the question of whether there is a true alternative often lacked a precise answer.

What is an alternative source? Within the industries I work in, you cannot simply ask "the Google" who else makes an alternator or an electronic component. These parts take years to develop. In-house engineers have customized them to the point where only one manufacturer can supply a particular widget. Even if several suppliers existed, the cost and time required to switch might be unacceptable. There are also potential stakeholders in your organization that will actively boycott and sabotage your attempt to bring in another supplier or product. (see graphic below).

Communication and Relationships

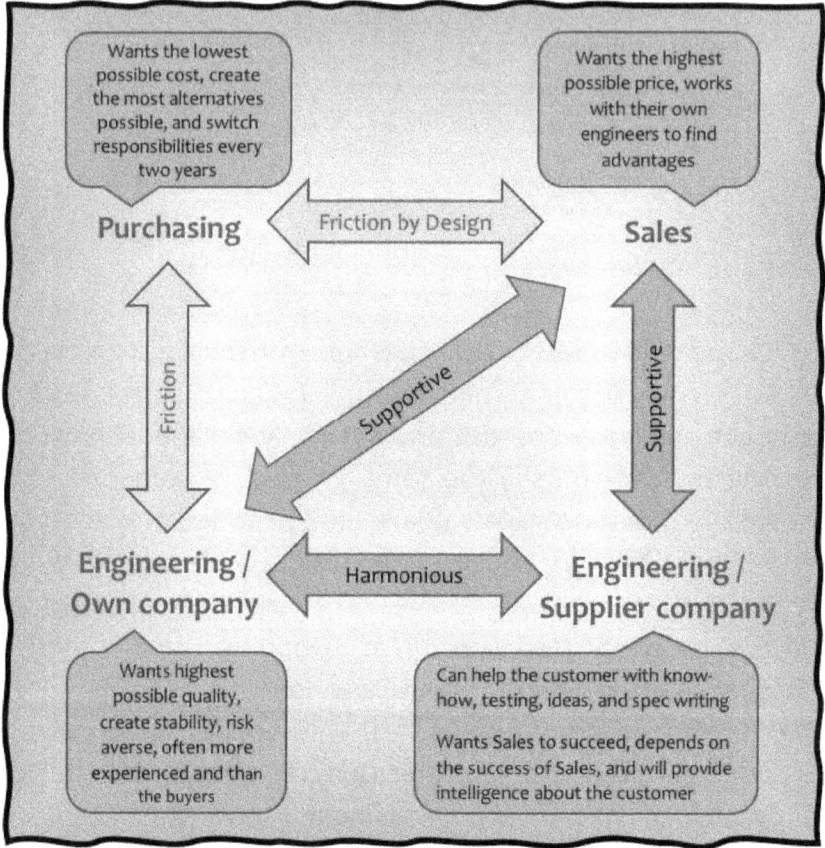

Figure 1: Communications and Relationships

Rest assured that even if you think you have a great idea for an alternative source, your Engineering, Quality, Finance, or Logistics Department can put a quick end to it. Get the necessary buy-in from your stakeholders before you threaten a salesperson with an alternative source. Those salespeople will activate their network, and *voilá!* They will find out that your Engineering Department never intended to sign off on the other supplier. Poof. No alternative.

This is not to say that there are no alternative suppliers available to you. I hope that there are. If you have many, you might even stop reading right here, because a good result should be easy. Make sure, however, that you check off these important elements of a good alternative source:

Do-you-have-a-real-alternative? Checklist

✓ Has Engineering, Quality, Finance approved the alternate supplier or product?

✓ How fast can a switch be implemented?
    ☐ Does that work with your timeline?
    ☐ Do other stakeholders agree?

✓ How expensive will the switch be?
    ☐ Do you need to buy new tools?
    ☐ Transport racks?

✓ Are there any risks to production and quality associated with the new supply?
    ☐ Can you accept those?
    ☐ What are they?

Once you evaluate these basic questions and you are sure that you understand the costs, risks, and timing involved, then you have a viable alternative.

CHAPTER 4: Faking an Alternative

Okay, time to discuss some risky business. What if I checked all options for leverage and bargaining power and there simply are none? Can I fake an alternative? Having spent most of my life in sales and executive management, I assure you that I have been confronted with a fake alternative at least a hundred times. Most often they come as a cheesy proposition, so transparent that all it elicits from me is a tired but knowing smile. If your counterparts have done their research, they will know whether it is true, especially in industries where alternatives take years to develop. We will discuss the topic of lie detection in the third part of this book. Having to lie, in fact, makes faking an alternative even harder, since, as you will see, most of us are not good at lying. By the way, that's a good thing!

This is what usually happens: You announce a fake alternative to your supplier. The salesperson calls his engineer who, remember, is bound to help his company's sales to be successful. The engineer also has a great relationship with the product engineer in your company. A few phone calls later, your Engineering Department, likely not even knowing that you are playing games with the supplier, confirms to the supplier that, indeed, there is no alternative. The best outcome from your ruse is that you just lost whatever remaining bargaining power you had. The worse, but most likely outcome, is that you eliminated the possibility of using the only strategy available if you are in a weak bargaining position: Partnership, based on trust and transparency.

Death of a Fake Alternative

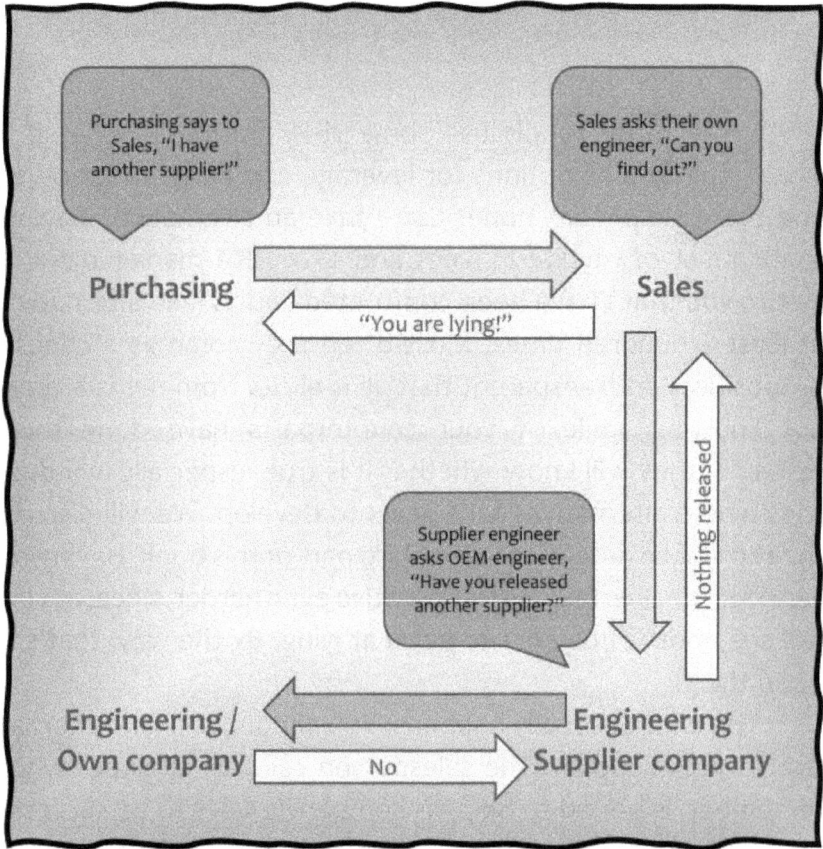

Figure 2: Death of a Fake Alternative

Remember, faking an alternative is the absolute last resort for a negotiation. It is high risk. If it fails, there can be serious consequences. It also takes a lot of preparation work. So, to be sure, I only use a fake in the most desperate and rare occasions.

I was once successfully 'faked'. I was a young salesman for a North American automotive battery company, and my biggest customer was a high-end German car manufacturer, an OEM with a production facility in the US. We had succeeded in creating a specification with the OEM's Engineering Department that made us the only source for batteries in hot climate markets, such as the US, Japan, and South Africa. We had effectively created a monopoly using the "harmonious" relationship between our engineers and the OEM's (see Figure 1 Communication and Relationships).

Although we did not abuse our position within the OEM's supply chain, I was aware of the strength of my bargaining position. I had given tiny discounts of one percent and less over the past two years. Now, it was time for another annual price negotiation in Germany. Self-assured and with another one percent discount in my pocket, I made my way across the Atlantic. When I arrived at the Administrative Center of my customer site—that was where the Purchasing Department was collocated with Engineering—I registered at the front desk. Instead of the buyer, whom I expected to greet me, the engineer responsible for batteries came for me. Franz was a familiar face and we had a warm relationship. He asked me to join him briefly in the basement where he had a small test lab. Franz mentioned that he had tested a few batteries and cut them open. He wanted to show me the failure modes.

When we arrived at his lab, Franz walked ahead of me. The lab consisted of two rooms. The first contained large water containers to the left and right of the walkway. These water containers served as temperature simulators in long-term cycling tests. Basically, the batteries sat in the water and the water temperature mimicked cold and hot climates. The test determined how often a car could be started in a specific climate before the battery failed. The second room into which Franz was now leading me was a small shop with a work bench and tools. Here, batteries that had finished the cycle test could be taken apart to analyze failure modes.

As I walked behind Franz, I noticed four batteries in a cycle test that had the words "hot climate" written on their lids. Hot climate? I immediately did a double-take. These were not our batteries! Franz had already gone to a workbench in the other room, so I had no choice but to follow. My head was spinning. Had Franz developed an alternative to our hot climate battery? I could certainly find out—if I had time to call my engineers and start some inquiries. But it would not be today. Franz showed me three failure modes with just enough time to spare to rush upstairs and make it on time for the Purchasing Department price negotiations meeting.

My alarm turned into panic when we arrived in the conference room on the fourth floor. Usually, the buyers were tough; no smiles, no platitudes. This time it was the opposite: The two buyers welcomed me with big fanfare, offered coffee, smiled, and made small talk (unheard of among Germans). They sat across from me, smiling confidently. At this point I was sure that they had developed an alternative, although they never mentioned it. They asked for a five percent discount. After a bit of back-and-forth, I gave in at two and a half percent. That was the most I had ever allowed, but with this OEM providing sixty percent of my business, I could not take the risk of losing the account. My job depended on this customer.

It was years later, while I pursued other ventures, that I reconnected with Franz by chance. He had come to visit another supplier in a nearby town and decided to contact me. Franz, Bob, our head engineer, and I had spent time fishing on a nearby lake on occasion. Since Franz stayed in a hotel over the weekend, I offered to take him out on the lake. So, Saturday morning, I hooked up my small fishing boat, filled the cooler with some sandwiches and beer, and picked Franz up at his hotel. We had a splendid time, talking about the good old days, common friends, and mutual colleagues. The topic of the price negotiation a few years back came up during the conversation. Franz laughed so hard that tears streamed down his cheeks. "We got you good that time!" he exclaimed. "You should have seen your face!" I had never seen him laugh like that before. I had to join in. "What did you guys do?" I asked.

Still sobbing, Franz told me the story of how, two weeks before my arrival for the negotiation, the buyers had come to him and asked for help. "We have nothing on Harry," they complained. "Can you help?" Franz came up with an idea. He went to a gas station and bought four batteries, removed the labels, took a sharpie, and wrote "hot climate" on the lids. The buyers were in on the fake, of course. Franz knew that I, the nosy salesman, would surely notice the batteries he had placed conspicuously into the water containers. All three buyers guessed I was scrambling to change my approach, based on what I had discovered just before I came into the conference room. And they could hardly keep from laughing. I had been had!

But I am not angry at all. I love good planning and execution. Franz never lied to me, neither did the buyers. The fake included clever time constraints and well-placed assumptions that did not give me time to do more research. A well-deserved win on their part! See? No lives lost, just a few points off my company's profit statement.

What is the most important lesson here? The communication and relationship between Purchasing and Engineering departments is critical. In this case, the buyers worked closely with the engineer to wrest a greater discount with the further purpose of keeping me, the supplier, in check.

Let's remember from Figure 1, Communication and Relationship, how the contact between Purchasing and Engineering is often fraught with tension. Engineering wants a stable supply with high quality parts. Maybe the engineers even have a favorite supplier that they have been dealing with for many years, who helps with development projects, and who does not generate quality defects. And along comes the new buyer, who just started the portfolio, and wants to switch suppliers. You can now understand that the engineer has a lot of power—often passive aggressive—to thwart the buyer. That kind of friction is wasted energy, and is internally damaging to any company.

My advice, especially to new buyers, is this: Get to know your engineers. Take them to lunch. Ask them pertinent questions about the product. Believe me, engineers are proud of their work, and when they are not overworked, are immensely helpful. If you have a price dilemma, for example, and you have established a good relationship with your engineer, you can form the argument this way: "I know you like your supplier. I appreciate their value. But, unless I can get the supplier to be competitive, I cannot sign off on buying the parts or allowing the supplier to bid on future projects. Help me find a way to keep the supplier! This is what I want to do…" Do you see how this approach is the best, and only way to fake an alternative? You must control the communication and preserve the relationship.

CHAPTER 5: A Mountain of Claims

I spent a lot of time coaching buying teams on tough negotiations as I mentioned in the introduction. When I say tough, I mean against highly sophisticated companies whose salespeople were aware of their bargaining power. The most annoying and destructive roadblocks I encountered many times were supplier claims, chargebacks, interest payments, inventory adjustments, and engineering changes. Were these claims for additional credit or payment valid? I've seen all kinds: justified, not really justified but negotiable, and outright fraudulent.

Buyers switch their responsibilities in the automotive industry every two years on average, as I noted in *Figure 1*, Communication and Relationship. Perhaps it occurs less frequently in other industries, but nonetheless, purchasing has a high turnover and many companies don't want their buyers to get too familiar with their suppliers by design. It makes sense to preempt even a whiff of conflict of interest, but there are serious downsides to switching portfolios too often. One drawback that I have found is that buyers will delay dealing with supplier claims—especially if they know they will abandon that portfolio in a short period of time. The result is that these claims linger on, sometimes build interest and value until the day they become useful in a price negotiation. That is a management issue. And, to be fair, I have seen suppliers skillfully build up a mountain of claims just before the next big negotiation.

So, here we are. We cannot negotiate effectively because the supplier insists on getting paid for the outstanding amounts of these claims first. Once I dig into what the claims are, I often find that somewhere way back, there was a valid complaint. Maybe engineering asked for a change without purchasing approval, maybe something as unnecessary as a missing digit on a bank account number prevented invoices from being paid and accumulated interest. There are many reasons for making claims. But there are not as many reasons for ignoring them. A minor financial dispute now stands in the way of a multi-million-dollar negotiation.

The sad truth is that you now have two negotiations to conduct: First, get rid of the claims, but in order to do so, you need to identify the validity, find the money to pay for them, and only then are you free to attack the second, more important negotiation. Don't fall into the claims trap and let the supplier use this leverage against you. The petition may not even be legitimate because the supplier has used your inactivity to build up a claim that is fraudulent. I have seen this not once, not twice...

CHAPTER 6: How is the Weather?

I wrote this chapter for my German friends in particular. I come from a culture where small talk has little value. Most Germans consider it a waste of time, superficial banter that does nothing toward advancing a deal. This chapter has two purposes: If you do not know how to make small talk, you will have to prepare that for your negotiation. Also, if you deal with Germans or people who dismiss small talk, be considerate. We just can't help ourselves. Having a beer with us after a tough confrontation, though, Is a different matter. See, we are not that bad.

Why would anybody engage in small talk? There are many reasons. The most important is that if you are not pursuing a pressure strategy but rather are trying to create a win-win situation, the relationship between you and your counterpart is important. You have to come to a mutual understanding where both parties are giving something up. Both are compromising. That requires an attitude of cooperation, a good measure of appreciation, respect, empathy, and trust. Establishing this atmosphere takes time and effort—and for most Germans—even planning. Most importantly, while creating this atmosphere, you should not engage in topics of the actual negotiation. Enjoy the small talk!

Is there a distinction between good and bad small talk? Absolutely! I am a big proponent of good small talk. When it turns superficial or boring, my German-ness takes over. I cut the small talk short. There are topics that have no place in any professional conversation, such as politics, religion, sex, sexual orientation, race, or any subject that could be sensitive or offensive to the other side.

Good small talk requires some preparation and research. Can you determine if you and your counterpart have things in common that are helpful in establishing a relationship? Details about your counterparts are available from co-workers, professional networks online, online search engines, social media, and previous negotiations. Good small talk shows interest in the other party. If you share a hobby with your counterpart, great! Share your experiences and, most importantly, let the other side share theirs.

I have played drums in rock bands most of my life. I never achieved any fame, but I still love loud music, playing in front of audiences, the teamwork in a band environment, and the creative process of writing and conceiving of music. I also love the challenge of figuring out patterns and rhythms. And, as a drummer, I sat far enough in the back of the stage not to get hit by things the audience was throwing at us (borrowed from a Ringo Starr interview). Countless times I have found out that my counterpart in a negotiation played an instrument. Within minutes we were engaged in deep discussion about music, the band experience, audiences, and such. We liked and respected each other completely outside of our professional environments. How had I found any of this out? Google searches and social media.

Let's consider other examples for good small talk topics. Many people engage in sports, or in the sports of their children. Competitions frequently find their way into the Internet, for example soccer tournaments, tennis championships, marathons, and martial arts competitions. These are easy to find. If you share a common sport with your counterpart, you have a great topic for small talk.

For the couch potatoes among us, there are great small talk topics in hobbies like reading books, watching movies, and following major league sports teams. Where is that information? People often share those interests freely in social media—even on professional networks.

Stay away from bad small talk. We all know the forced, "How is the weather?" or "Did you find a parking space?" type of small talk. You'll likely get little more than a yawn in response. However, there is even worse small talk. It has to do with how you present your research. You should be subtle. Ask questions that lead the small talk to where the other side feels comfortable enough to open up.

Crudely blurting out what you know can have the opposite effect. Imagine a salesperson starting with "I looked you up on LinkedIn and…" Or, "So, I hear that you like sailing…," clearly referring to a photograph in which you are tagged in Facebook. See, what happens now? Instead of sharing a common interest, and using that to get to know each other better, the feeling of empathy can easily turn into the opposite. Creepy! A cyberstalker! A troll! I personally do not like it when people invoke my family and personal life in professional conversation. That's just me. Why would you care about my personal life? Once you broach the subject overtly, my answers likely will be extremely short. Maybe I'll even become angry, and the whole purpose of the small talk will have been ruined.

When I discuss the topic of small talk and how to prepare it in my training seminars, I sometimes look the participants up online. Usually, they are shocked about how much information I can find in a matter of a few minutes. But I also learned to be careful with that. I gave a seminar a few years ago in Detroit. I found out that one of my participants played in one of the best-known bands in the region. He played lead guitar and vocals. I was excited. We had the great love for music in common. Great example for discussing small talk topics in class, I thought. The information had not been easy to come by. The participant used a stage name, and the only clue that connected him to his band was a photograph on Facebook, in which he was tagged, probably without his permission. I matched it with his LinkedIn headshot and had what I needed.

When we met in class, I casually mentioned that I played in a band and looked at him. Dead silence. Showing a complete lack of sensitivity on my part, I mentioned his band's name and how much I liked their music (It was good! I had found a live cut on the band's website). He blushed and stammered something about a stupid, unimportant hobby. As I found out later, the participant in my seminar had kept his nightlife a secret from his colleagues for three years. He was afraid to be associated with sex, drugs, and rock 'n roll, because he worked in the financial services sector of his company. I had accidently publicized his carefully kept secret! I feel bad about the incident to this day. Since then, I always privately ask participants before the seminar if they would mind me mentioning something I have uncovered. That was definitely an example of bad small talk, albeit unintentional and innocent.

There are few rules of engagement to consider:

Rule #1: Never let the other side know everything you know. Casually throw out a keyword and see what comes back.

Not, "I hear that you like sailing...," obviously gleaned from a dated Facebook post when a friend tagged me in a photo without permission. How about this: "One of my best friends lives in Charlotte, North Carolina. His house is on Lake Norman. Last weekend he took me out with a J/24 (a small two-person sailboat). It was so much fun!" Let it sit. If nothing comes back, the small talk topic is obviously not productive. Drop it. However, most likely the other side will offer something like their love for sailing. Now you have a good conversation starter.

Rule #2: Never fake interest in a hobby! If you don't play golf, or have no idea about sailing, or music, please don't fake it. The other side will take you for an imposter immediately because you don't know the right jargon.

Is small talk important? I had this discussion countless times with my German clients. We will see later in the book when we discuss strategies that if you do not start a negotiation with small talk, you are signaling that your strategy is pressure. If it is, no problem. But if it is not, you have just negatively influenced the upcoming negotiation.

I learned my business skills in the American South. As a perceived outsider... There might be people around today who knew me in my 20s and 30s when my negotiation skills were rough around the edges that might describe me as rash, scathing, or overly ambitious... The worst part of these character descriptions is that I perceived myself to be tough but hard working, friendly, fair, open-minded, big-hearted... If you believe that perception is reality, then my reality certainly was not that of my counterparts. I had to work on this cultural dilemma for many years. Now that I am accustomed to the ritual of small talk, my German counterparts, who are not, actually offend me at times with their cutting directness. I had to actively prepare and practice good small talk. If it does not come naturally to you, then you may want to practice, too.

One last item about small talk: How long should it last? Under a pressure strategy, it can, and should be, short. However, if you are pursuing a win-win strategy, small talk needs to be longer. I often ask in my training seminars, "How long should small talk last?" The Germans in the room say one to two minutes. It could last fifteen minutes or longer for Southerners. Chinese negotiation partners would like to have dinner the night before to have enough time to get to know one another. In my experience, cultural norms seem to be a strong influence. So, how long is appropriate?

Rule #3: Small talk lasts as long as it takes to make the other side feel at ease and relaxed. Yes, it could be a whole night or fifteen minutes. It could also just be five minutes. One or two? Unlikely, unless you negotiate in Germany.

Chapter 7: Dependencies

One of the most underestimated but critical questions that defines the starting position involves dependencies. How dependent am I, and how dependent is the other side on a result in this negotiation? The easiest way to look at dependency is to focus on the relationship between your purchasing volume and the total revenue of the supplier: What are the gross sales of the supplier? How much of that is my purchasing volume? One percent? Ten percent? Fifty percent? As a rule, anything over ten percent is significant and shows a high dependency. Ask your Finance Department for up-to-date financials and credit information. Public companies have to publish their results, so look online for their annual reports. If you are lucky, you may find that the company in question provides financial data split by division, region, or product group. All of that will help you determine how much your purchases mean to the supplier.

There are other measures of dependency that are not so obvious. I once coached a negotiation for an OEM in a country that values social responsibility. The OEM is one of the smaller players in the automotive world, but successful on a global scale. This particular negotiation had to do with purchases of brake parts from a large, global supplier.

When I met the team on a cold winter morning, I asked the members to present the case to me. All they described was doom and gloom! After about an hour of evaluating the background of the case, I was ready to give up. The supplier had all the power. Switching these parts to another supplier was not impossible, but expensive and time-consuming. Worse, the supplier salesperson seemed very aware of his power, deriding my buyers for even suggesting a cut in price. I heard quotes like, "This is too low volume to cut cost," and, "You are lucky we can even keep this price." Finally, "Take it or leave it!" *Take it or leave it?* That made my blood boil, and in the third part I will discuss how to maintain your cool. It is essential for negotiating.

So, we started digging into the data to find leverage. We checked all the numbers, service levels, purchasing amounts, global sourcing—nothing. After some exhausting few hours, I asked one of the buyers, "Where are these parts made, and where are they used?" I knew that the supplier had multiple production facilities in North America. My idea was simple: Could there be a dependency based on location? Sure enough, that was the root of the issue. The supplier produced all the parts for the OEM in one facility. Even better, the supplier had located that facility right next to the OEM's factory. Sixty percent of the production capacity went to the OEM. Dependency? You bet! I immediately started plotting with the team on how we could threaten the supplier by pulling the orders and shutting down the production site.

I mentioned earlier that the OEM has its headquarters in a country that values social responsibility. Well, that nixed any leverage. My buyers looked at me in horror when I suggested the argument. They would never agree to do that—and the supplier knew it. Yes, culture is also an important part of the equation.

I encountered an interesting dependency once that is still relevant in the automotive industry today. The development of electric cars and self-driving technology brings suppliers to the table that are new to the automotive industry. Imagine, an executive in one of these companies is maneuvering to enter the automotive industry. He or she identifies one specific OEM, maybe BMW, which is looking for cutting-edge technology. Once the OEM signs up, the door would be wide open to use this automotive customer to acquire customers in the rest of the industry. Daimler, VW Group, and Fiat-Chrysler are now within grasp. How important is it for that executive to win this first automotive customer? You bet! Very important. Is there a dependency? Absolutely! It is a strategic dependency. As a buyer, you had better look at your suppliers' business plans or persuade them to present their market strategy to you. You might just be the chosen 'gateway' customer! How do you find out? Invite the supplier to present their company and business plans. More often than not, suppliers will volunteer their strategic vision.

Dependency also exists on another level that many buyers often overlook. Buyers are paid a salary. Maybe they receive a small year-end bonus. However, that is not true for their counterpart salespeople. Commissions generate large portions of a sales income. Across industries, the variable income of sales forces in companies is anywhere from 30% to 60%. Salespeople in some industries such as real estate, or the secondary car market, depend 100% on commissions for income. It is worth researching how your salespeople are compensated. If you have a key account manager call on you, try to figure out how many accounts they have. Are you their biggest customer? Do you think the result of the negotiation is important to the key account manager if you are? Imagine the possibility that the salesperson's ability to pay for their kids' college tuition depends on making the sale. Dependency? Very much so, but on a different level. The salespersons might negotiate on your behalf with their manager, if they believe a deal is workable.

CHAPTER 8: Who is coming?

The quality of interpersonal exchanges between two sides determines the outcome in any human interaction. Yes, you heard me correctly. Bringing a negotiation to a successful conclusion depends mostly on factors that are not necessarily logical, financial, or even sound business practice. Factors such as motivations, personality preferences, culture, stress levels, and many more seemingly unrelated factors determine the outcome of a negotiation conducted by humans. Wouldn't it be nice to know who is sitting across from us, what they are thinking, what motivates them, how they think, and what would make them agree with me?

I have a particular pet peeve that many buyers, and especially purchasing managers, have heard me complain about for over a decade. Why are we so inefficient in Purchasing at handing down supplier information from one buyer to the next?

My first gig in industry was to do market development in Eastern and Southern Europe for the largest polyester yarn manufacturer in the world. I had this job in the early 1990s, a few years after the Soviet Union had collapsed and Eastern Europe had opened its borders to the West. The job fascinated me. Nobody in the West knew anything about the Baltic States, Poland, the Czech Republic, Slovakia, Hungary, or Rumania. Suddenly these were all countries to which my company expected to sell yarn. We needed to know how big the textile industry was in each of these countries, what equipment the factories had, and if it was paid for. We had to find out to whom these factories were selling, and if they were financially stable. You can get an idea of the conundrum we faced. There was no Internet, no Google, not even Dun and Bradstreet. Nothing. We just did not know.

I started in Poland, the largest textile market in the former eastern bloc. Someone gave me a lead on a professor at the textile university in Lodz who could be a potential sales manager for the country. I contacted him, made an appointment, and flew to Warsaw. I met Professor Stanislav and hired him on the spot. Apart from the fact that he had the best credentials of any country sales manager I could have found; he was also kind and dedicated. His father had flown for the Royal Air Force during World War II. Stan had grown up in London and spoke English fluently. So, off we went in Stan's little Fiat. For months we crisscrossed the country, going from factory to factory. As I had imagined, Stan knew everyone. Most buyers had graduated from his classes sometime in the past. Also, all these managers across Poland knew each other and many were friends, because in the old communist system there had been no competition, just a plan.

I started assembling and analyzing the information I collected on a Microsoft Excel spreadsheet. I categorized factories by number of employees, type of machines, production capacities, as well as customer and supplier base (my competitors). I did not stop there. For every company I took down the names of the managers, their education, time on the job, work responsibilities, name of their secretary, and anything they volunteered about their personal lives. Stan, of course, also remembered the managers from when they were his students.

Some were better students than others and I could tell from Stan's diplomatic characterizations who they were.

After a six-month period selling nothing, but just driving around and leaving free samples everywhere, I had an impressive array of information. I had created my own credit system. I had figured out what yarn products fit in which factory, who my competitors were, and how much they charged for what. I had become acquainted with just about everyone in the industry. Wherever I went, I brought thoughtful little gifts, I remembered birthdays of managers (long before Facebook!), and I asked questions about my clients' hobbies, kids, and their communities.

I genuinely cherished my new group of customers, though my descriptions may appear calculated and manipulative. The individuals I grew to know and respect were some of the most impressive entrepreneurs I have ever met in my professional life. These men and women took over huge, decrepit factories of four to ten thousand employees, with on-site schools and kindergartens, on-site shops, and gyms. These factories were not just production sites. They were little cities, fully equipped to serve all their workers. Under communism, there was no unemployment. The government paid for everything.

Now these new entrepreneurs had taken over the sites, had to close down all the social facilities and appendages of the factories, and streamline production and equipment. Operating with only a few hundred employees, they now produced more than four thousand had before. Many did exceedingly well, and, in the process of their success, local economies sprang back and flourished. It was a pioneering time that, to this day, I am grateful to have witnessed.

The biggest challenge for these new manufacturers was how to find customers. Under the communist era five-year plan there were no customers. Moscow needed red socks, so you made red socks. If, six months later they needed green socks, you made green socks. Customers? Marketing? Unheard of.

I tried to help as much as I could. I showed samples of western European fabrics and brought in buyers from large clothiers in the UK, Germany, and France. My strategy worked. Within a fifteen-month timeframe I sold my yarn all across the country. We became the number one yarn supplier in Poland.

This case illustrates how success is often based on valuing people. I learned a lot about the people with whom I was dealing and wanted to do business. In his book, *Beyond Reason*, author Roger Fisher makes the important case that perhaps the most important tools of the trade spring from relationships. Today, CRM (customer relationship management) software tools make sure that a sales organization collects and maintains detailed information about their customers. What we typically do in Purchasing is move our buyers to new commodities every two years. Often, we move them into a new department on the other side of the globe. How much relationship information remains after the buyer leaves? Not much. It would behoove major Purchasing Departments to employ 'supplier relationship management' tools, as well.

But lacking such a tool, you and I have to do this ourselves. If I prepare a negotiation, I want to know as much as possible about the other side. Below is a helpful checklist. Consider the possibility that virtually all sales organizations worldwide may have assembled this same data on you.

Supplier Relationship Management Checklist

✓ How much experience does your counterpart have?
✓ How committed are they to their work?
✓ Where did they work before?
✓ What hobbies/sports do they enjoy?
✓ What is their personality preference?
✓ What is their negotiation style?
✓ How easily do they come under stress?
✓ How do they behave under stress?
✓ In which culture did they grow up/are they living in now?

This is a checklist to help you find this information:

Personal Information Source Checklist

✓ Has a co-worker in purchasing, engineering, quality control, or logistics negotiated with this supplier?
✓ Does anyone in your professional or social network know the salesperson?
✓ Does the salesperson have public social media information (Facebook, Twitter, WhatsApp, Instagram, Tumblr?
✓ Does the salesperson have online resumes that are public (LinkedIn, Xing, Monster, Indeed)?
✓ Does Google return information on the salesperson?
✓ Does the salesperson have published work online (scholarly articles, blog, books)?
✓ Does the supplier publish information on their sales staff?

Let's assume you have done your homework and you checked all of these sources. Please do not do anything unethical while gathering this information. I am completely opposed to faking a personality online; moreover, it is also illegal to hack, or otherwise steal private information. We may only use public information in our work. If it shocks you how much you can find out about someone, you may want to consider tightening your own privacy settings on social media.

CHAPTER 9: Robbing the Bank

W hen I debrief negotiators after an exhausting session, the frustration is often palpable. I hear characterizations such as "stubborn," "pig-headed," "uncooperative," and worse. That might actually be true in many cases. But in just as many cases, the negotiators had not answered an important question while preparing: Is the person on the other side able to decide? We all know from experience that in many negotiations we do not have the luxury of facing the final decision-maker. As a matter of fact, all automotive companies with which I have worked have decision-making committees. The final word on any deal the buyers bring to the table rests with senior management.

So, the obvious question is whether or not you can negotiate without the decision-maker in the room.

'No,' you might say? Not so fast. If you knew before the negotiation that the decision-maker was not coming, then you could have prepared for that. Certainly, you would have had to make some changes to your approach. If you do not have the decision-maker in the room, you have to build in extra time for your counterpart to go back to their company and get approvals. You might prepare documents for your counterpart that help argue your case. They could take those back to the boss. The key here is the fact that you need to know if you will have the decision-maker at the table. If you don't, you might falsely accuse your counterpart of all the bad behavior I mentioned above.

No, the salesman is not stubborn, arrogant, and uncooperative. He is not allowed to say "yes." No matter how much you badger the poor soul, the result will be no decision, maybe even worse, an *éclat* and unnecessary personality conflict.

How do you find out who the decision-maker is?

I remember a coaching session during which the team adamantly reported to me that the counterpart was uncooperative, arrogant, dismissive, and rude. That did not sound good. The supplier, just like the OEM I was coaching, had operations in both Europe and Asia. The purchasing team wanted to combine the global purchases in a deal to achieve more leverage. However, the supplier refused any attempt to bundle. It makes sense, of course, that most suppliers would try to avoid that.

After some back and forth, I asked if the team was talking to the decision-maker. Well, yes, they replied in a chorus. He is the Vice President of Sales of the company. Why would he not cooperate? We decided to go online and check the company website. Under 'About Us' there was an organizational chart. Sure enough, there were two vice presidents of sales, one responsible for Europe, the other for Asia.

As with most issues related to business, people typically do what they get paid to do. The Vice President of European Sales, with whom the buyers were talking, derived no benefit, maybe did not even have the authority to help with bundling Asian and European sales. He had been uncooperative—maybe even arrogant and dismissive—because my team had been talking to the wrong person. The organizational chart showed a Senior Vice President of Sales under whom both VPs worked. *He* was our guy. Not long after our meeting, the buyers I had been coaching closed on a good deal with their supplier, sweetened by the bundling of global purchases.

While it is possible in many cases to negotiate with someone who is not authorized to decide, the goal should always be to get the decision-maker to the negotiating table. That is easy to do in smaller companies. It is often next to impossible in large corporations. When I was in sales, I used a strategy that often worked. I called my customer and gave them the exciting news that my boss or boss's boss would be visiting from Europe or the States and wanted to have a meeting. I left it at that. My purchasing counterpart then scrambled and told their boss that I was coming with a senior manager. The purchasing manager now felt compelled to join the meeting or bring an even higher-up to the table. *Voila!* I won. Now, I had the decision-maker at the table.

The role of the decision-maker in a negotiation is critical and cannot be compromised. Nobody knows more about this than former hostage negotiators who worked for the German federal police like Matthias Schranner, or for the Federal Bureau of Investigation (FBI) like Gary Noesner and Christopher Voss. Both Schranner and Voss are now successful negotiation trainers and speakers. These are not people just working for a company and trying to make an extra buck for their shareholders. Hostage negotiators are highly trained specialists who, if they would fail, could cause people to lose their lives. The stakes are infinitely higher.

Here is one of the concepts that the FBI developed that helps to illustrate the role of negotiators, supervisors, and managers in a negotiation. Imagine the following situation: A man with a hood covering his face runs into a bank. He fires his gun into the ceiling. "Everyone on the ground!" he screams as he runs towards one of the cashier windows. Some of the customers manage to escape through the door. One of the bank employees also manages to press the alarm button under his desk.

The bank robber finally gains control of the bank. He locks the door. On final count, he has three customers, a man, a mother with her ten-year-old daughter, and two bank employees, both female. The rest of the employees had slipped out of the employee side entrance of the bank.

Police arrive and block off the roads around the bank. One of the officers interviews a customer who had just escaped from the bank building. He describes the situation inside the bank: The bank robber was armed and dangerous and had hostages.

The local police department has to call in the FBI in the case of a hostage situation. A negotiation mistake in a case like this could cost lives!

The FBI comes to the scene and immediately takes over the pizza parlor across the road from the main entrance of the bank to create a command center. The command center has two functions: A commander manages the situation on the ground and communicates with higher-ups at the FBI. A highly skilled negotiator, often with extensive psychological training, is in charge of direct contact with the bank robber. Profilers, tactical leadership, investigators, and a host of other supportive staff also could be in the command center. For this purpose, let's just look at the commander and negotiator. The commander can listen to the conversations between the bank robber and the negotiator but is not allowed to speak. The only person allowed to speak with the bank robber is the negotiator, and only through a secure phone line.

I always pause when I use this example in a training session because I want students to think about it, even though the answer is predictable:

"What would be the first thing the negotiator might ask the bank robber?" I ask.

"What do you want?" The buyers usually respond.

No, that is not the first question! I understand, in business, we are trained to put humanity aside and maximize shareholder value no matter what. Hopefully, in a case with lives at stake, the first question would be something like, "Is everyone ok? Is anyone injured inside the bank?"

Sooner or later, the negotiator certainly will ask what the demands are as the conversation with the bank robber continues. The negotiator might also ask, "Why are you doing this?"

Imagine the bank robber saying, "I lost my wife and son in a car accident three weeks ago. I have nothing to lose."

Here is an important question for you to answer about the negotiator: Looking at this negotiation from an objective level, do you think that it is possible that the negotiator could be emotionally attached to the negotiation?

No, you might respond. He is a professional, highly trained psychologist.

Okay, I agree. But can you be sure that the negotiator did not lose his wife or child sometime in the past and empathizes with the emotions of the bank robber? Or, can you be sure that the negotiator had to deal with a similar bank robbery in the past, and the criminal at that time brutally executed women and children? Could the negotiator feel hatred and disgust towards the bank robber? I am not saying that any of the above is necessarily the case, but remember, the risk alone is already too much to take because people's lives are at stake here.

Let's talk about the commander. She is not actively speaking with the bank robber. But the same questions apply: Is she potentially emotionally attached to the negotiation? Be careful with your answer. She, too, could have lost a loved one, or harbor other feelings about the bank robber that could cloud her judgment.

The answer for the FBI is clearly that both the commander and the negotiator could be emotionally compromised in this negotiation. Therefore, the decision-maker is not on the ground. He is on the third floor of the J. Edgar Hoover building in Washington D.C., in a corner office with a window. He receives periodic updates from the commander. He also has command over the tactical team whose sharp-shooters have taken up positions on the rooftops around the bank. One of the snipers has the bank robber in his crosshairs, waiting for the word...

Bank Robbery with Hostages

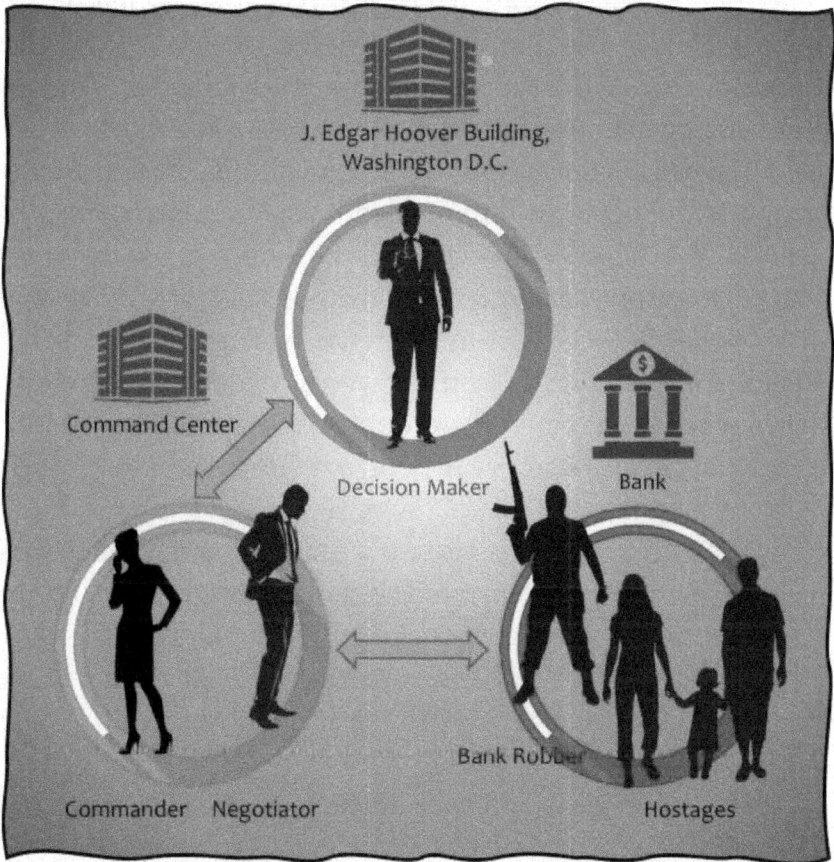

Figure 3: Bank Robbery with Hostages

When the negotiator asks the bank robber what his demands are, the answer comes back that he wants a million dollars and a helicopter to fly him to Mexico.

Does the negotiator have a million dollars and a helicopter to give? Of course not. Does the commander? Nope. The only person in this scheme who has a million dollars and a helicopter is the decision-maker. He also has the ability to have the bank robber killed.

What does the negotiator have to offer? Pizza. In fact, after a few hours of talking with the bank robber, the negotiator asks if the people in the bank are hungry. The bank robber, himself starving, exchanges the woman and child for pizza. The last male customer and the bank employees remain as hostages.

The negotiator continues his work, making more and more progress. Suddenly, the entire negotiation turns into chaos. The bank robber hears a siren close to the bank and assumes that the FBI is getting ready to storm the building. He screams into the phone, "I will shoot one of the hostages every fifteen minutes if you don't call off the assault team." The situation becomes dire. The bank robber does not accept the explanation that what he had heard was a benign firetruck responding to an accident on the other side of town.

The commander reports to the decision-maker what is happening on the ground. Just as the decision-maker picks up the phone to order the tactical team to kill the bank robber, the negotiator manages to get him to back down. He commits to the negotiator that he will not harm the hostages. That was close!

Imagine what would have happened if the decision-maker had been in the command center and actively participated in the negotiation. There are some gruesome examples, in which that was the case. Three people, a law enforcement officer, Randy Weaver, his wife, and his child, died in exchanges of gun fire during a standoff with the FBI at Ruby Ridge, Idaho in 1992. Four Alcohol, Tobacco and Firearms (ATF) agents and eighty-two cult members, many of whom were children, died in the siege of the Branch Davidian compound near Waco, Texas in 1993. Tactical assault teams sidelined the negotiators in both cases with devastating results. In the case of our bank robbery example, the negotiator succeeds after hours of hard negotiation at getting the perpetrator to release all the hostages and give himself up. No one is injured.

Now, let's transfer this scenario to our daily work. You are a buyer in the purchasing department of your company. The bank robber is the salesman, the negotiator is the buyer, the commander his immediate supervisor. I call him the coordinator. The purchasing manager is the decision-maker. Imagine the scenario in which the buyer spent weeks preparing for this negotiation. He carefully executes a cooperative strategy. The coordinator is fully briefed and makes sure the negotiator has all the resources he needs. The purchasing manager receives periodic updates from her. The buyer allows time for several meetings so that the salesman can coordinate with his superiors.

As the negotiation drags on, the purchasing manager becomes impatient. Why is this taking so long? He asks the coordinator to tell the buyer to hurry up. When the buyer spends hours in yet another meeting with the salesman, and they still have not reached an agreement, the manager has had enough. He comes to the meeting room where the buyer and coordinator are negotiating with the salesman. He slams his fist on the table, demands a discount—or else the supplier gets fired.

Imagine this situation!

Role of the Decision Maker

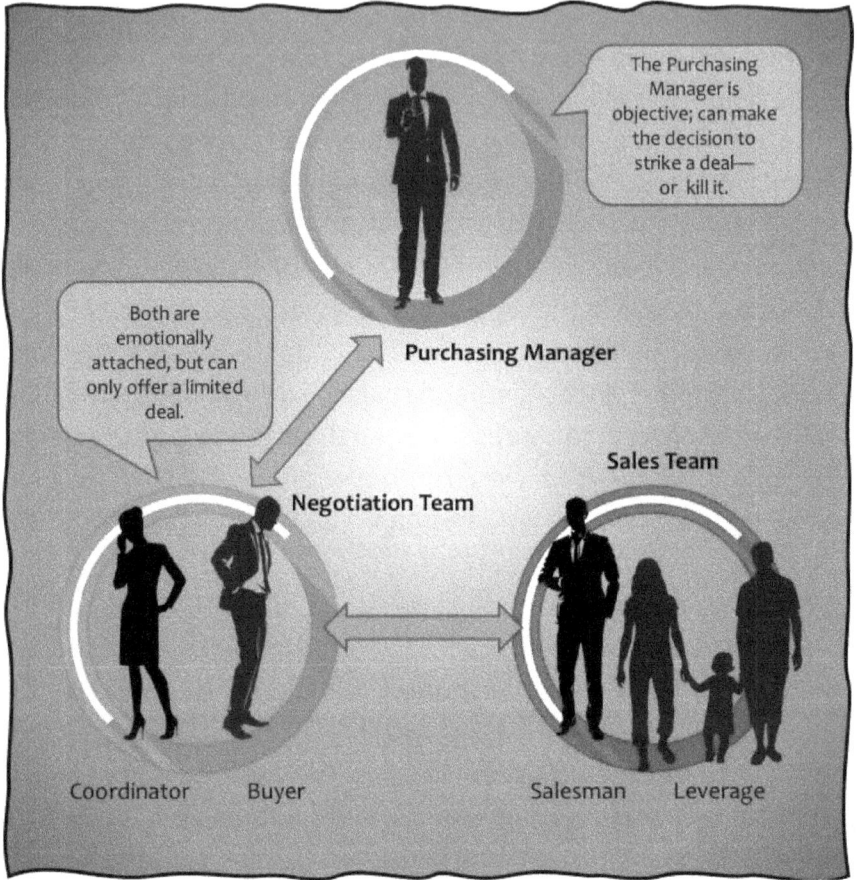

The Purchasing Manager is objective; can make the decision to strike a deal— or kill it.

Purchasing Manager

Both are emotionally attached, but can only offer a limited deal.

Negotiation Team

Sales Team

Coordinator   Buyer

Salesman   Leverage

Figure 4: Role of the Decision Maker

Do the buyer and the coordinator have a million dollars and a helicopter? No.

Does the purchasing manager? Yes. In fact, he is who the salesman really wanted to talk to all along.

How much preparation time has the purchasing manager spent on this negotiation? Not too much. He has dozens of simultaneous negotiations to oversee.

How familiar is he with the strategy and tactics the buyer and coordinator were pursuing? Not very much. He received periodic updates on the progress, but not on the actual negotiation.

How much power do the negotiator and coordinator retain, now that the manager is in the room? None. The purchasing manager is now in charge of actively conducting the negotiation. His two employees are watching his every move. "How is he going to do a better job than us?" they wonder.

Is the purchasing manager under pressure to make a deal? You bet. He feels pressure to save face in front of his employees and the salesman. He now also needs to make a deal quickly since he interrupted the process because of his impatience.

The situation is not good. The purchasing manager has a million dollars and a helicopter. He is ill prepared and under pressure to succeed. He's lost his objectivity. Worse, the salesman, who is highly experienced and well prepared, can withstand the pressure and fist-banging of the manager. He understands his position. The bank robber's hostages are now the leverage of the salesman. The purchasing manager applies pressure but, suddenly, he realizes that he does not have enough leverage. So, he makes a deal to save face. It's a bad deal. I am not saying that this is necessarily the outcome, but it is a highly likely scenario.

I have coached many purchasing managers over the years who were overloaded with work. Why? Think about this: Why would a salesperson ever call on a buyer if the manager were accessible? So, after inserting himself once into a negotiation and handing the sales team a better deal than they could have received from the buyer and his coordinator, the salespeople from now on will knock on the manager's door. Multiply that by the amount of important negotiations happening in the purchasing department and *voilá*! You have an overworked manager, employees who are not empowered, and the results are bad.

Let me go back to my past as a devious salesman.

How does the negotiation team deal with someone like me who brings senior managers into the negotiation? Quite simple: don't allow it. Just say that your manager does not have time. Or, even better, get your manager to come by, shake hands, say a few friendly words, have them empower you with a compliment, and then have them leave the room. Now, that is a strategic and good negotiation technique.

We are now clear about the role of the purchasing manager in a negotiation. What about the sales manager?

The tables are now turned. You, the buyer, want to get the sales manager to the table. The sales manager has the million dollars and the helicopter, he is under peer pressure to succeed, and he might be ill prepared. You have the chance to get a great deal.

Getting the Decision Maker into the Room

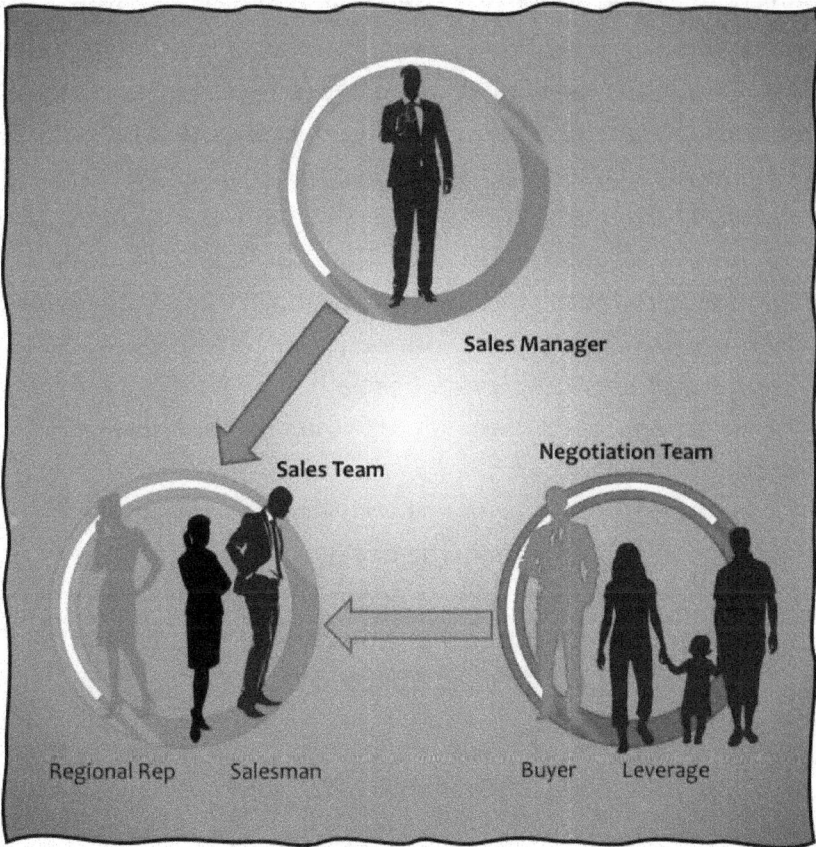

Figure 5: Getting the decision Maker into the Room

Simply use the strategy that I described earlier. You create the same ruse. Tell the sales team that your boss will be there for the meeting and would like to meet the sales manager. The salesman will likely try to bring his manager along for the meeting. Then, if it works, use the purchasing manager's role briefly, either as the proverbial baseball bat who comes in, threatens the sales manager, and then leaves; or, as the nice guy who enters the room with a big smile, shows interest and appreciation, and then leaves the room quickly. In the first case, you now have a perfect good guy-bad guy setup. The purchasing manager leaves, and you can apologize for your boss. The sales team might not want to meet your boss again and prefer to make a deal with you. If your boss is playing the nice guy, and leaves after some pleasantries, you also have an interesting situation. In this case, the sales team knows that they are expected to do well. That the big boss is paying attention to the result of the negotiation. All these tactics work, as long as you do not allow your manager to take away all your power and desperately try to make a deal.

Here are the rules about the decision-maker in a negotiation:

1) In general, never reveal your decision maker. Let them stay informed but remain in the background.

2) If you are organizing a negotiation, always try to coax the decision-maker of the other side into the negotiation.

3) If you are a manager, empower your negotiators, don't intervene unless there is a clear strategic advantage.

CHAPTER 10: Personality Matters

When two people meet each other, two distinct personalities interact. That simple understanding has a huge impact on negotiations. Not only is it important to recognize how personalities influence any negotiation, but also how conflict can erupt, and how to manage it. I will discuss much more of that in the second part of this book. Important in this part, where we discuss how to prepare a negotiation, is the question of whether I can anticipate reactions from the other side and prepare for those. Would it not be great if I knew what personality types I would be facing; what motivations they may bring to the negotiation table?

There are many personality-preference models in the marketplace. While psychologists have scoffed at some of the less scientific models, the idea of personality preferences evolved from research in transaction analysis (more about transaction analysis in Part 3). Transaction analysis tries to determine the expected reaction to an impulse. How do we make decisions? According to psychologist William Marston, we decide from looking at four poles: Am I perceiving the environment as advantageous or disadvantageous? And, am I more powerful or weaker in this environment?

This four-pole paradigm developed into personality preference models that tried to predict the decision-making process of distinct personalities. Myers-Briggs was the model of choice when I was a student many years ago. Individuals answered a questionnaire that placed them into a combination of four final pairs of preferences: extroverted or introverted; intuitive or sensing; thinking or feeling; and, judging or perceiving.

Sometimes, I use a model called DISC in my training seminars. It separates people into four preferences: dominant, influential, steady, and conscientious. Similar to DISC is the Color Code personality test, using four colors to describe similar archetypes.

The German model, STAB, also has four archetypes (Structure, Trust, Action, and Relationship), and addresses the same behavioral patterns as the previous two.

A favorite model that I discovered some years ago is the Passion Profiler, a system that separates people into ten preferences and gives a self-reflection score. It is the most thorough and scientific personality preference model on the market, but too complex for the purpose of creating a simple tool for negotiations. If you would like to understand your personality preferences better, and how to enhance the productivity of your team, this is the model I recommend.

Psychologists have adamantly opposed the oversimplification of personality that can lead to flawed interpretation and misuse. Science is still not able to define exactly what creates personality and whether innate, definable personality preferences explain behavior. Therefore, I am presenting a tool that works for predicting what are likely motivators, and how the other side might react to my arguments. I am not attempting to define personality from a behavioral science background. Think of it as a filter that helps to quickly compartmentalize the other person with whom you are interacting.

This is, by the way, what your brain routinely does. We compare and contrast the signals from another person with our experiences, cultural understanding, education, and memories. We have to make these comparisons in order to prevent our brain from overloading with signals. We feel sympathy or antipathy anytime we meet a person—even for the first time—and this feeling is immediate. Is it fair? Can prejudice and discrimination cloud our judgment of the other side? You bet. I passionately believe that the more we try to predict and prepare how our counterpart will act and react, the more we can suppress prejudice and negative emotions that may cloud our judgment and affect our interaction. I have used my understanding of personality preferences for decades in every negotiation I prepared and conducted. Personality preference models are tools that help me as a negotiator, and hopefully, they will do the same for you.

I will describe four basic archetypes that are present in most models. You can choose any one of the previously mentioned models to determine your own personality preferences or, you can study my descriptions. Most likely, you will recognize yourself pretty easily. I am intentionally simplifying them here with the understanding that behavior and personality are vastly more complicated. For the purpose of this book, I want to answer these basic questions: Which of the four personality preferences do I rely upon? Which preferences are the person sitting across from me relying upon? How can we, as two distinct personalities, arrive at an agreement? I am very keen on making the distinction between the façade, which is the way a person manipulates behavior to appear a certain way to others, and the true person without the influence of the environment on their behavior. Finding that true person will further understanding of the decision-making process, the reactions of the other person, motivators, potential pitfalls, and sources of conflict in the interaction.

The Scientist

The Scientist represents detail orientation. This personality searches for knowledge, is precise, and risk averse. Scientists strive for perfection as their main motivation. Dedicated to finding even the most obscure detail to help solve a problem, these personalities are self-motivated and work hard. They address a challenge with data and evidence. The Scientist is able to assemble data and facts into a structure that is logical in order to solve a problem. They avoid direct conflict in their interactions with others. If conflict arises, Scientists, if they are empowered, will defend their findings and conclusions. They prefer to retreat, however, when facing their superiors, or when they otherwise lack authority and power. Usually, they devote more time to conduct more research and look for a solution to the conflict in the data.

Since Scientists spend a lot of time alone, they may appear socially awkward. Their communication skills are better written than verbal, the latter often not precise enough for them. That does not mean that they are not friendly and cooperative in a team environment. This archetype is respectful and diplomatic, especially in their interaction with authority. Scientists are always prepared, and most of the time know way more than they lead other people to believe. This archetype is always willing to search for a new approach if supported by the data. Scientists engage in trials to find the perfect solution. They are willing to change their opinion if the data supports it, but only then, because taking a leap of faith is not in their nature. They are utterly risk averse.

The colleagues at work might not respect or understand this personality type. Scientists are often viewed as slowing things down, taking too much time, and being timid about making leaps of faith. This, in turn, might prove to be a problem because a Scientist is sensitive and, therefore, vulnerable when it comes to how they are treated. Scientists may appear arrogant, disengaged, seemingly hedging their bets, and not willing to make decisions, especially because they are not good communicators. In reality, Scientists might just be overworked. They strive for perfection which is never really achievable. So, The Scientist keeps working without ever being done.

Decision-making is definitely a data-driven process that requires careful convincing, facts in support of the decision, and time. Others might interpret this process as a deliberate effort to hold up the progress of the team. Under pressure to make a quick decision, The Scientist withdraws or, if pushed into a corner, becomes stubborn, arrogant, or dismissive. The previously snubbed Scientist may well say that they knew all along that it would happen in situations when the team failed.

They can be most persistent in areas where they are experts. In every other topic outside their area of expertise, Scientists change their opinion if their environment changes. They are susceptible to peer pressure and social influence for this reason. Their level of confidence is fed by their intimate knowledge of the facts, not so much by firm opinions and social support. The perfect place for The Scientist in the team is to make use of their uncanny ability to take seemingly unrelated facts and assemble them into a logical structure. As long as this archetype has the time to do the work, and as long as the team accepts the need for data and research, The Scientist is a truly valuable asset for the team's efforts.

How do I recognize The Scientist? Look for their level of preparation. Scientists will think of any eventuality. They will carry with them their own notebooks, or extra tools. Their desks might be messy, but they will know exactly where to find anything in that space. The appearance might not be particularly fashionable or may even appear sloppy, like sporting a worn-out belt, or having a conspicuous stain on their jacket. If this personality engages in social media, they will have very few friends. Hobbies include anything having to do with detail, such as reading, collecting things, restoring old houses or cars. Vacations likely will be based on gaining knowledge and sightseeing, rather than adventure and social interaction.

Characteristics of The Scientist:
- Strives for Perfection
- Asks critical questions
- Analyzes
- Concentrates on facts
- Dislikes negative reactions and conflict
- Decides slowly
- Specializes

THE FARMER

The second personality preference is The Farmer, and it stands for process orientation. Think about how Farmers see their world as one divided into clearly delineated farms and fields, about which they know everything. They are not interested in the neighboring farms or fields that are not part of their farm.

Farmers want to make sure that everything on their land works flawlessly. They understand the rhythm of nature, the quality of the soil, where there is water and where there is not. Transcribe that to the workplace. Farmers are the people that make the business run smoothly. They understand and support processes. They know exactly how things work within their area of responsibility.

Farmers are calm, consistent, and friendly teammates. A well-functioning team fulfills their deepest quest. They want others to understand the environment in which they work. They identify with the team, the company, their environment. Farmers are loyal by nature. Friendships are long-lasting, as are marriages, and other social affiliations.

The biggest enemy of The Farmer is change. Change is disruptive. Predictability and stability are their main motivators. A new farm and new fields mean a lot of extra effort to gain the thorough understanding of how things work and how to make them efficient. By nature, The Farmer is conflict-shy and so the resistance to change manifests in passive aggressive behavior.

While ostensibly diplomatic and agreeable, Farmers are sensitive and vulnerable. Personal life remains strictly separated from professional life. They respond to conflict with process-based arguments of why something cannot work. During times of turmoil or change, this archetype appears to be pedantic and pessimistic. It will take an especially long time to forget and forgive when managers or coworkers offend or mistreat The Farmer. They will not seek the open conversation to settle a conflict, but rather remain angry and offended to the point that they themselves suffer mentally and physically.

Farmers respect rules and make process-based arguments. They will ask questions about when a meeting will start and how long it will last. The need for predictability will make them uncomfortable in a new environment or when new information surprises them. The road to a goal is just as important as the goal itself. If the goal is outside The Farmer's domain, they will delegate quickly to let higher-ups deal with a problem. The decision-making process centers on the process and the rules. Does the goal fit into the established process? If not, The Farmer will refuse to cooperate, and either escalate the problem to someone above his pay grade, or engage in passive aggressive maneuvers to undermine a decision they really do not accept.

How do you recognize The Farmer? Look for team-based hobbies that are not dangerous, such as soccer or basketball. They like vacations to be well planned and predictable, such as cruises, Club Med, or pre-arranged tours. Farmers probably do not travel alone, but rather with their families or friends, and often to the same place year after year. Farmers will be punctual and friendly but reserved in a meeting. If confronted, they will retreat into a shell of rules, especially when they are alone, making it impossible for you to reach an agreement.

Characteristics of The Farmer:
- Seeks harmony, safety, predictability
- Adheres to rules and procedures
- Dependable, punctual, and disciplined
- Dislikes when their boundaries are not respected
- Good team player
- Hates change

THE MERCHANT

The Merchant takes the place of the great communicator, the personality that sees a win-win situation almost anywhere. They are the dealmakers, the people who use their networks and relationships to scope out the common ground. Merchants are flexible and open-minded. This archetype has an uncanny ability to establish contact, and convinces others with their enthusiasm and optimism.

Merchants want to be liked. In fact, this motivation is so pronounced, that at times they hide their opinions and agree with others against their own convictions. This characteristic can make them appear superficial in extreme cases. Their inherent optimism and enthusiasm also cause Merchants to fall into the trap of promising too much, of overestimating their own ability to deliver. Merchants will use their charm and communication skills to extricate themselves when caught in an embarrassing situation in which they have overpromised and underdelivered.

Merchants are well liked and popular in a team environment. Their pronounced idealism and enthusiasm energize their teams. However, their great flexibility to make a deal often collides with rules and procedures, as well as facts and established knowledge. Anything is negotiable! The natural role for The Merchant in a team is to communicate within the team, on behalf of the team, and to the outside world.

Merchants decide quickly and from their gut. Deals have to feel right. This distinct approach to decision-making can cause serious frustration with all the other personality types. If a deal feels right, The Merchant's idealism allows for a leap of faith.

How do you recognize Merchants? This archetype receives energy from other people. Merchants are very social and always surround themselves with others. They are great communicators, interested in others, and therefore ask lots of questions. Among this group of personalities, you will find artists, entertainers, salespeople, and promoters. They dress fashionably, prefer casual to formal meetings, and prefer to pick up the phone and call you before writing a memo or sending an e-mail.

Characteristics of The Merchant:
- High level of interpersonal skills, high enthusiasm, very sociable
- Team-oriented and communicative
- Decisions are made on gut instinct
- Dislikes criticism
- Puts people before goals

THE HUNTER

The Hunter is a go-getter, a natural leader who makes things happen and basks in the glory of eventual success. Hunters seek out a lofty goal, a trophy deer with huge antlers. They will stalk that trophy relentlessly for as long as it takes. The Hunter not only takes the meat when he finally succeeds in slaying the animal, but cuts the antlers off, and mounts them behind his desk on the wall so that the whole world can admire how big that deer truly was. Trophies and the glory of success are their main motivators.

Hunters are highly motivated, committed, and hard workers. They also expect everyone around them to work just as hard. Once they set a goal, they will pursue it without looking back, even if the team is lagging behind them. Any means to the end is acceptable while in pursuit of that goal. This attitude causes friction and conflict around this archetype. Hunters act quickly and decisively. Unlike other personalities, Hunters like to take significant risks, especially if the prospect of a large reward looms on the horizon. Problems that appear in the pursuit of the goal can be solved along the way. People, rules, data that stand in their path become obstacles and must be removed.

The Hunter rarely takes prisoners. Compassion is weakness, while tenacity—even in the face of hardship—is virtue. Competition defines them. They live in a world of stark black and white contrasts: winners and losers, leaders and followers. Hunters enjoy the jousting and power-play that ultimately carries them to leadership positions. Obstacles arouse their ire. They hate to give up or change their goals. They may appear impatient, arrogant, ruthless, and unyielding to others. Hunters always are aware of their power and use it ruthlessly. Lacking power, they buckle down until the time comes when they can take charge. It is important to them that the world perceives them as successful. Not being able to save face in a negotiation will make an agreement next to impossible.

Hunters are easily bored. Change is a requirement for progress. Standing still is equivalent to losing ground. Once hunters reach a goal, they will immediately search out a new one. This can be exhausting for their teammates. If they do not succeed in reaching their goals, they easily blame others, maybe even change their team and their 'hunting grounds'.

How can you recognize The Hunter? Hunters are direct, competitive, and don't shy away from conflict. They will take charge naturally and immediately if you let them. Interested in how the world views them, they surround themselves with trophies: the expensive car, the luxury vacation, the beautiful wife, the newest iPhone. Hunters dress expensively and fashionably. Appearance and prestige are especially important to them. They pursue competitive sports, preferably where they are in charge. You will find this archetype in tennis, golf, the striker in soccer, or the coach of a team. Vacations often involve risk and adventure, or prestige and class. Hobbies may include piloting small planes, rock climbing, martial arts, and boxing.

Characteristics of The Hunter:
- Everything is a competition
- Looks for challenges
- Needs fame and recognition
- Collects trophies
- Fast-paced, impatient
- Born leader, difficult team member
- Wants to win, hates to lose
- Risk-taker

Have you found yourself in some of these descriptions of archetypes? Remember, these descriptions are purposely simplified. There are very few people who display only one personality preference, but rather a combination. What happens, for example, to people like me, who are a mix of Hunter and Scientist? War inside my head? No. These preferences are complementary. For example, I set ambitious goals for myself, like writing this book—a daunting task. But because of my detail orientation, I also have done a lot of research and I have convinced myself that the goal of writing this book is achievable and realistic. What about a combination of The Merchant and The Hunter? Similarly, the hunter preference will propel that person into setting lofty goals, working hard, and removing obstacles. The Merchant, however, allows that same person to communicate effectively, possibly being much more capable to motivate the team than a hunter could do without also having that second preference as a trait.

Which personality preferences do you think will create the most successful team? All hunters? Hardly. All Scientists? This, too, would make for a highly dysfunctional team. You would see lots of research and data but no decisions, no results. The answer is all of them. A team that functions well must include all of these preferences. But wait! There is another critical ingredient: The team members have to be open to the fact that everyone is different. We all come from different places, make decisions in different ways, and we are all motivated by different things. If we can accept that, and have all the preference archetypes present, then this will be a well-functioning team.

One of the most important distinctions to draw in the evaluation of personality preferences and the resulting motivations, decision-making processes, and negotiating styles is the so-called façade. The façade is the public personality, the outward appearance of a person. We all modify our personality preference based on the social environment, our team at work, or our position in the company. The work environment causes us to pump up or push down certain personality preferences. For example, if I (and this is a fact) do not have much of a Merchant preference as part of my personality, how could I successfully teach seminars or share anecdotes? It seems counterintuitive. This is where the façade comes into play. I can consciously pump up my Merchant preference. I can learn to communicate and appear to others as if that was my natural preference. Well, it is not. But I am surprisingly good at it.

So, what does that mean? A Merchant wants to be liked; a Scientist wants to gain knowledge. These are two distinct motivators. A Merchant also decides from the gut, while a Scientist decides from evidence and data. These are diametrically opposed decision-making processes. And this is why understanding someone's façade is absolutely critical. Although I, as a Scientist, can put up a pretty convincing façade of being communicative and social, I still make my decisions based on facts and data and never from the gut. If you interpret my façade as a hint of how I make decisions, and appeal to my emotions for a decision, you will never convince me.

Throughout my years of coaching managers, I have found that in most companies a manager is expected to be tough, decisive, and goal oriented. I have often witnessed an absurd power-play in management meetings where a horde of hunters commingles, resulting in trophy comparison and tough talk. Those are façades for the most part. Not every manager is a pure hunter. They might have a good portion of that preference as a trait, but I have found many detail-, process-, or relationship-oriented personalities. Without knowing the real individual, the true personality preference of these managers, I also cannot know on what they base their decisions, what motivates them, or, for our purpose, how to get into their heads and make them agree with us.

Another important fact to understand about the façade is that it takes energy to pump up one preference and subdue another. Since I am not a natural communicator, I am exhausted after eight hours of doing my best in a training seminar. I will go to the hotel, grab a book, eat in the room, and recharge my batteries in peace and quiet. A true Merchant would still be energized and, instead, go to the hotel bar, connect with the people there over a beer, and keep talking. I don't know how they do it, but then again, they don't know how I could write a history book with a thousand footnotes. We are different.

Ultimately, we all tend to gravitate to a role in our work environment that best utilizes our true personality preferences. I have found through my years of coaching that the longer people work in a company, the more likely their private and their professional personality preferences become the same. The façade fades away.

The façade is work-related. I gave some hints about how to recognize the different preferences of the four archetypes at the end of each description above. The true personality preference comes out in private. Hobbies, vacations, and private social behavior tell the real story. Imagine a hunter who works on a production line in a factory. He has nothing to think about except how to install that radio in a truck dashboard. What will he do when he gets home? Most likely, his hobbies and his social life will reflect the balancing of the work and the private life. He will play competitive tennis, run a local club, and collect trophies.

Let me put you into a hypothetical situation with each of these personalities and explore how they act. This exercise will help you identify and recognize the different archetypes. Let's say we are all going on a cruise. Why would the different personalities go on a cruise? What would they do on board?

The trip promises to be great. The ship will cruise through the Mediterranean Sea with stops in Greece, Israel, and Egypt. While on board, there will be lots of activities to do between stops. The cruise liner offers all kinds of live entertainment, music, theater, stand-up comedy and more. A large dining room hosts the daily evening gala. Dinner is included in the price of the cruise. There are also multiple restaurants on board, some very reasonable, others quite expensive, where you can either stop for a snack or have dinner apart from the other guests. If you like sports, you can play tennis, swim in the two large pools, try your skills on a climbing wall, or play miniature golf. A casino and several bars, one with a nightly karaoke program, round out the offerings on board.

The cruise line offers multiple sightseeing options for the stops in Greece, Israel, and Egypt. For example, the ship plans to dock in Alexandria for the stop in Egypt. From there, you could either join a group that is bussed to the pyramids, or you can hire a guide who will take you there and give you a personal tour. Alternatively, you could book the adventure tour. This includes a private drive into the Sahara, and a camel ride through the desert with a group of Bedouin nomads that will take care of all your needs.

Imagine that you are The Scientist. Why are you excited to be on this cruise? Well, you have a bucket list of places you always wanted to visit. The Acropolis, the Holy Land, and the Pyramids. And all that in ten days! What a deal! Always the researcher, you have read up ahead of time. By the time the ship docks in Alexandria, you will have brushed up on all there is to know. Which option for visiting the pyramids and the Sphinx will you choose: group, private guide, or camel ride through the desert? Option number two, of course; the private guide with a personal tour. Not only can you tell the guide what you want to see, but you can also lecture him on all you know about the pyramids, the Sphinx, and Egyptian history. The group travel is wholly unappealing. Lots of people in a confined space, sweating…

As a matter of fact, that is also the downside for the entire cruise. You wish there were less people on the ship. Whenever you have the opportunity, you sit in your cabin, porthole open, and read while listening to classical music. You only go to the large dining room at dinner time because you already paid for the food. You try to find a table with only a few people seated.

Sometimes, the other diners at your table are interesting, and you make some conversation. Most of the time, however, conversation is limited to pleasantries, and you turn to see what is happening on the stage.

Day three of the cruise is exciting for you. You ask the chief engineer if you could see the engine room, and he gives you a tour. Wow! What great technology this ship has! There are high capacity tanks with huge pumps that can move large amounts of water from one side of the ship to the other within seconds. This is why you hardly ever feel waves or movement on the decks.

As a Farmer, you are not too keen on traveling. The vacation at home, and finally having enough time to tend the garden, is much more appealing for you. You have two favorites among the vacations you have spent away from home over the years: Taking your Recreational Vehicle to the familiar spot in the mountains of New Mexico and taking a cruise. You can visit all these different places without ever having to change your room. Additionally, the schedule is clear, and the excursions that you booked months in advance, are fully planned. The trip promises to be a great one. The ship has updated safety features and you made sure before booking the trip that there were enough lifeboats on board, and that your cabin is not below the waterline. In fact, your cabin is right next to a lifeboat, which makes you feel good. You booked the trip with your neighbors in Chicago, where you live. This is the fifth cruise you're taking with them. You even manage to reserve the same table you had the year before, right next to the doors—in case there is a fire and you need to make a quick exit.

There is a lot to do on board. The neighbors' kids are twelve and ten. You take them to play a few rounds of miniature golf every day. They're sweet kids, very well behaved. When the ship docks in Alexandria, you all take the bus with the other passengers to the pyramids. What a sight! The tour stops in Cairo on the way back. Some passengers scour the markets and sample all kinds of local food. You don't because there are some nasty bacteria in the water here and you don't know if the food will make you sick.

You are a Merchant and you love cruises! Why? What an opportunity to meet people! You have ten days to get to know 5,000 passengers. And, who knows? Some of them might be great connections for your sales job. Networking is everything. The ship is loaded with amenities. There are so many things to do that you don't know how to do all of it in just ten days. There are concerts, theater performances, and your favorite: Karaoke. The days on the ship are full of activities. You hang out at the pool and have happy hour at the pool bar. There is even a strip of beach for playing volleyball. You meet a great group of guys on the second day of the cruise: one from New York and two from San Francisco. It turns out that the Californians actually work with an old college friend of yours at an investment bank. Small world!

The excursions are also incredibly interesting. You ask a group of tourists at the Acropolis if they want you to take a photo of them. As you get into a conversation with them, it turns out that they are also passengers on your ship. What a coincidence! Dinner is great, the dance afterwards even better. Wednesday night there is a story-telling competition in one of the theaters. You just happen to walk by, see the sign and decide to go in. What an unbelievable stroke of luck! You not only walk in there completely out of the blue, but you tell this story about your brother's second wife—and you win the competition! Well, it was a great story. There simply are no hours to waste. Sleep? Maybe when you get back.

You hop on the bus to the pyramids once the ship docks in Alexandria, and you have a blast at the market in Cairo on the way back. You have never seen so many different fruits, dates, tangerines, mangoes, grapes, whatever exotic fruit your heart desires. You even show some of the guys on the tour how to eat a prickly pear. They love it. You will probably keep in touch with them, a nice group of friends from Atlanta.

For a Hunter, cruises are not necessarily the favorite vacation choice. Were this not the maiden voyage of the largest cruiser ever made, you probably would not have been interested. But here you are, in a first-class cabin overlooking the bow of the ship, with a stunning view of the ocean melting into the seemingly infinite horizon. No one on board has better views other than the captain in the helm, maybe. The cabin is spacious, and you also have a large balcony. Right after the ship leaves the berth in Barcelona you post some incredible photos on WhatsApp, showing the size of the ship and the views. Life is good.

You paid a lot of money for this cruise, but luxury has its perks: You get to sit at the captain's table two nights in a row. One of the restaurants on board has two Michelin stars. Expensive, but you plan on winning in the casino later on, then spending the money on a culinary adventure with your wife. While most passengers get on dirty busses and swarm Athens, you take the opportunity to play a round of golf. Your club membership in Kiawah Island allows you to play on some of the most prestigious golf courses in the world, including the number one course in Greece: The Glyfada Golf Club of Athens.

Life on board of the ship is not too boring, either. Every morning at six you go to your favorite breakfast bar, then you work out on the pool deck. Not many people are around yet, other than those who are working out, as well. There is one guy, about your size and height, who has impressive biceps. Definitely an encouragement to continue the weightlifting! By the end of the ten days, you want to look better than him. The rock-climbing wall is quite a challenge. Every afternoon, when the sun is not blasting that side of the ship, you work on your skills. There is a blue track up the wall. That is too easy. But the black pegs, those are the ones not everyone can climb up on.

There is only one excursion choice that you even consider when the ship docks in Alexandria: The camel tour to Giza and The Valley of the Kings. What could possibly go wrong? Who cares that only last week there was a terrorist attack on the Sinai Peninsula? That was hundreds of miles away. The Bedouin guides know what they are doing. Has anyone ever gotten lost in the desert on one of these excursions? You don't know and you also don't care. Let's go and hopefully live to tell your friends about it when you get back. Supposedly, you get a camel hair wallet that says, "Sahara Ride of the Century" on it.

What do you think? Cruises must be fun. Well, I wouldn't know because being a Scientist myself, I have no interest in spending a week cooped-up with thousands of people.

Archetypes

Scientist:

- Strives for Perfection
- Asks critical questions
- Analyzes
- Concentrates on facts
- Dislikes negative reactions and conflict
- Decides slowly
- Specializes

Farmer:

- Seeks Harmony, safety, predictability
- Adheres to rules and procedures
- Dependable, punctual, and disciplined
- Dislikes when their boundaries are not respected
- Good team player
- Hates change

Hunter:

- Everything is a competition
- Looks for challenges
- Needs fame and recognition
- Collects trophies
- Fast-paced, impatient
- Born leader, difficult team member
- Wants to win, hates to lose

Merchant:

- High level of interpersonal skills, high enthusiasm, very sociable
- Team-oriented and communicative
- Decisions are made on gut instinct
- Dislikes criticism
- Puts people before goals

Figure 6: Archetypes

CHAPTER 11: When Two Personalities Meet

N ow that we have met the four personalities and understand them a little better, we need to see how they interact. What happens when one personality prepares to negotiate
with another? What are the pitfalls? Where are the sources of
conflict? How can one convince the other to come to an agreement? These questions are critical to a successful negotiation.

If you are using pressure as a negotiation strategy, then you
use your leverage, power, and position relentlessly to win
against the other side. The Scientist uses data and drowns out
the other side's arguments. The Farmer insists on their process
and rules. The Hunter confronts the other side and applies their
leverage and power ruthlessly. The Merchant... Well, The
Merchant hates pressure and certainly won't prepare a
negotiation with that strategy in mind. Given the context of this
book, winning against the odds, I am more interested in
situations where you want to cooperate with the other side.
Remember, negotiating from a position of weakness is the
challenge at hand. Almost any negotiator knows how to apply
leverage. Here are the things to consider for creating a
cooperative environment:

THE SCIENTIST MEETS ANOTHER SCIENTIST

A meeting of two Scientists will be about comparing and contrasting their data. That can take a long time, but when the process is finished there will be an agreement. Scientists can change their mind if the data of the other side is compelling. The pitfalls for a negotiation such as this are clear: The two Scientists get lost in the details, get distracted, and take way too long to come to an agreement. If you are a Scientist and you prepare this negotiation, create an agenda, limit the time to negotiate, and stay focused on the topic of the negotiation.

THE SCIENTIST MEETS A FARMER

The meeting between you, The Scientist, and The Farmer hinges upon two quite different approaches to finding an agreement: You, The Scientist, will assemble data and evidence to create a logical solution as the basis for the negotiation. The Farmer, being friendly and cooperative, will agree with you as long as you are still working within the fences of his farm. You do not necessarily see the boundaries of your counterpart's fields. You are willing to go where the data takes you. Farmers will check any solution against their rules and processes, and that poses a potential problem for the negotiation. Once you leave your counterpart's farm, once you propose a solution that does not fit within the habitual processes of The Farmer, you will lose them. Make sure that you understand the processes within which your counterpart is operating to prevent this from happening. Get to know their 'farm'. Then find a solution that fits within the requirements of the other side, and you will have a productive negotiation.

THE SCIENTIST MEETS A HUNTER

Scientists negotiating with Hunters is riddled with boundless pitfalls. These meetings often end in an éclat: The Hunter counterpart does not have the patience to evaluate The Scientist's research. Hunters want to act, to move, to decide. The common mistake of you, The Scientist, in these meetings is that you bring way too much detail to the table. Keep it concise, don't start with Adam and Eve to get to today's topic. Prepare an executive summary (yes, on one page!) for The Hunter to read.

In my first job as a management trainee in the Logistics Department of a polyester yarn manufacturer, my boss asked me to figure out whether our next generation fleet of tractor-trailers should be purchased or leased. As it turned out, this was not as easy as it sounds. I took three months to analyze the routes of our trucks, the movements of incoming and outgoing freight, identified fourteen distinct patterns, and applied cost accounting data to all of them. My calculations spanned a spreadsheet of more than 600 pages. The data showed that purchasing the fleet would eventually be more cost effective than leasing.

I knew I had to condense all that information to present my findings to my boss, who was definitely a Hunter. So, I created a three-page executive summary as the introduction to my study.

When we met, my boss laughed at the three-inch-thick report I brought, and immediately exclaimed, "I hope, you are not going to make me read all that!"

I was offended since I had put an immense amount of work and overtime into this study.

"No," I assured him, "I have an executive summary right here." And I handed him the three pages. He scanned the first page, went to the next...

He suddenly looked up.

"Buy or lease?" he asked abruptly.

"It's on the next page," I murmured.

Too late. I had worn out my welcome.

"Look," he said, handing me the study. "Come back with a one-page summary. I want to know whether to buy or lease. That's it."

I was crushed. How would he ever understand the method I devised to come up with the solution? The more I brooded over this rejection, the more I wished I would have stayed in my history PhD program. I hated the thought of having to work with people who had the attention span of one page. What kind of decisions do people like that make?

It took me years to appreciate what my boss actually conveyed to me. He trusted me and did not need all the details I presented because he knew that I had done my homework. He just wanted the solution. As a Scientist, I just did not get that important message: Keep it pithy!

Also remember that The Hunter is direct, can be aggressive, and has no problem dismissing all your hard work. Hunters will cut you off, interrupt your train of thought. Expect this from The Hunter and don't be offended. When my boss laughed at the 600-page study, he had no idea that I took it as ridicule.

Let The Hunter appear to be winning something, show appreciation for the research over which they do have command (even if it might not be as precise as you wish), and, please, don't correct or interrupt them. Hunters make their decisions based on the glory of the achievement and how their success will be perceived by others. Let them take the glory, while you get what you want.

THE SCIENTIST MEETS A MERCHANT

The Merchant is a personality that you, The Scientist, not only don't understand, but often dislike. Merchants make their decisions from the gut. As a Scientist, you cannot understand that type of decision-making process. The biggest mistake you, The Scientist, can make, is to dismiss The Merchant as superficial and illogical. They just don't like to do much homework, so you have to accept that. Try to be respectful, even if they don't know as much as you do.

Don't make the mistake of assuming that The Merchant is following you when you present your data. While Hunters start yawning and looking at their watch if you present too much data, The Merchant remains attentive and seemingly interested. They are friendly and want to be liked. They will not try to offend you. But the reality is that your data just went in through one ear and out the other! Just assume this to be the case. Prepare your data and evidence in writing so that The Merchant can take it with them to wherever their detail-oriented people are. Also, increase your small talk. I know, you hate to waste time on small talk, but The Merchant needs it during your interaction to feel comfortable and connected.

THE FARMER MEETS A SCIENTIST

If you are a Farmer and you prepare a negotiation with a Scientist, you can count on a productive meeting. Just make sure that you explain the parameters of your work. Scientists can be in love with their research and, in the process, tend to leave the farm. Both of you are conflict-shy, which should make a constructive meeting easy to conduct.

THE FARMER MEETS A FARMER

Among Farmers, negotiation is not very confrontational. The two sides will take their time to explain each other's processes and parameters and then make a deal. Or not, if an overlap does not surface. Then, they escalate the negotiation to the higher-ups in their organization. As a manager, empower The Farmer to make it harder to escalate the decision-making process and promote a compromise agreement.

THE FARMER MEETS A HUNTER

If you are a Farmer, Hunters are your most difficult negotiation counterparts. Hunters don't care about rules and processes. You have to make sure you don't rouse their ire when you explain your processes. Be positive! Don't say, "This will never work, because…" Try instead, "These are the pieces that have to fall in place for your plan to work." Hunters don't want to hear "No." They want to explore with you how to reach their goals.

You, The Farmer, hate conflict and rapid change. Expect exactly that from your counterpart. Hunters are aggressive and you have to give them some leeway in that. Don't take their advances too seriously. Hunters sometimes confront people just to gauge their reaction. Let them appear to win. If they feel good about themselves, they are easily manipulated into an agreement that is good for you.

THE FARMER MEETS A MERCHANT

If you are a Farmer, then The Merchant is not hard to deal with for you. Merchants are friendly and cooperative. You just have to watch out that they understand the rules of the game. Merchants love to propose exceptions to the rules. Everything is negotiable for them, including your hard-and-fast rules and processes. Don't let them slip out of your boundaries.

THE HUNTER MEETS A SCIENTIST

If you are a Hunter, you have to work hard on interacting with any other personality. Especially The Scientist, a personality you loathe: Slow to make decisions, never done with the work, long-winded, and risk-averse. The fact is that Scientists might be the only people to prevent you from making a wrong decision. Listen to their evidence and logic. Scientists may be long-winded, but they think through a problem thoroughly.

When you prepare a meeting with a Scientist, do your homework! And if all the detail work bothers you, then bring a Scientist from your department with you. If you are unprepared, count on The Scientist to call you on it. Show interest in their work and don't interrupt them. If you break their train of thought, they will be offended and may stubbornly insist on their opinion. Be patient, appreciative, and convince them with your own data and evidence. Never expect The Scientist to say yes on the spot. Build into your preparation the possibility of several meetings, so that The Scientist has time to contemplate and feel comfortable with an agreement.

THE HUNTER MEETS A FARMER

The same applies to you, The Hunter, when you interact with a Farmer. Be patient, friendly, and cooperative. Farmers tend to be nice people, but they can drive you crazy with rules. You have to understand the confines of their environment, because a Farmer will not follow you blindly. Make sure you plot out the road to the goal, explain attainable intermediate goals, and lead The Farmer along. For heaven's sake, never use the proverbial baseball bat on The Farmer. They will remember that mistreatment for all eternity and your relationship with them may never recover.

THE HUNTER MEETS A HUNTER

The most explosive combination of personalities is in negotiations where two Hunters meet. Two strong personalities, who love the sparring, who hate to lose, who never give up... What could possibly go wrong? If you are a Hunter and you prepare a meeting with another Hunter, you have a lot of work ahead of you. Prepare a win-win strategy. Make sure the other side has the ability to save face. Dial back your ego. Give the other side small wins. If you have the possibility of bringing someone to the meeting, bring a Merchant. The Merchant can sense the first sign of conflict and will work hard on solving it. Going into a meeting with another Hunter has a huge potential for catastrophe. Build in breaks. Prepare good small talk. Admire the trophies of your counterpart. If you have a bigger boat that is more expensive than his, don't mention it!

THE HUNTER MEETS A MERCHANT

Hunters typically get along quite well with Merchants. Merchants want to be liked and are often accommodating and supportive. Make sure you explain your goals clearly and give The Merchant the task to work on your behalf with their boss. Don't be impatient when The Merchant talks too much. Accept small talk that does not necessarily appear to help you with your goal. The Merchant needs to relax. Don't be too quick to start the negotiation. Remember, Merchants are idealistic, self-motivated, and willing to take a leap of faith with you. Build up their enthusiasm. Get them to believe in your vision.

If you have the urge to spar, then The Merchant is the personality with the least amount of long-term consequences. You can beat up on a Merchant and they will be back again later to try once more to be liked...

THE MERCHANT MEETS A SCIENTIST

If you are a Merchant, please prepare your negotiation. The only way you can convince The Scientist is with data. They do not want to hear excuses. As a matter of fact, The Scientist will call you out on being unprepared, imprecise, or offering superficial explanations. Scientists are all about nuance and precision. If you hate doing all the detail work, bring your engineer along. Don't try to wing your presentation. It will not work. Also, dial back your small talk. If you must engage in small talk with The Scientist, ask them about their current research project. Don't pretend to know something about which you have no idea, even in small talk. Ask good questions and let The Scientist talk. Don't interrupt The Scientist during your interaction with them. They take their time to come to the point and that is okay.

THE MERCHANT MEETS A FARMER

For you, a Merchant, everything is negotiable, including rules. Not for The Farmer! You have to make sure that you understand the rules and processes of the Farmer. They will not compromise on those. The argument, "Just this one time..." will fall on deaf ears. Otherwise, you will have a good negotiation. Farmers are friendly and cooperative. Be on time! Stay away from personal topics in your small talk. The Farmer wants to talk about his department, his team, his company, not his sick wife or his hobbies.

THE MERCHANT MEETS A HUNTER

Here is your chance to shine. As a Merchant, you have all the tools to make The Hunter eat out of your hand. Stroke their ego. Admire their trophies. Let them have the feeling of winning. Respect their successes and hard work. Cut down on your small talk. Then you will make a good deal!

THE MERCHANT MEETS A MERCHANT

Here are two personalities in a negotiation that have a style no one else will ever understand. If you are a Merchant and you prepare a negotiation with another Merchant, then make sure of one thing only: Don't let your boss interrupt the meeting.

A good friend, who scores high on The Merchant scale, once shared a story. He is a consultant who lives in Germany and also teaches seminars all over the world, just like I do. When he first started his consulting career, a small business owner with 500 employees in a nearby town in Germany called him and asked to book some training seminars. The owner was a lady in her late 30s, and genuinely nice on the phone. It was immediately clear to my friend as they chatted that she was very much a fellow Merchant. They agreed to a meeting the following week. Two days before the meeting, the business owner called him and asked to postpone. Her husband was turning forty that Saturday and she was busy planning a big birthday bash for him. My friend agreed to a new meeting the week after.

When they finally met in person for the first time, guess what my friend asked as his first question? "How was the party? And, by the way, I am turning forty later this year myself. I have no idea yet what I will do for a celebration." Forty-five minutes of conversation ensued. About what? The party, of course. After forty-five minutes, the lady looked on her watch.

"Oh boy, I just realized how much time went by. I have an important meeting in five minutes. What are we going to do about the seminars?" she asked.

Within five minutes, the two arrived at a deal.

Here is my question: How long did they negotiate? Fifty minutes or five? You might have guessed right. Fifty minutes. Merchants negotiate through seemingly unrelated conversation. They check out the other side's position, detect their willingness to compromise, and determine the potential for an agreement. When my friend and the business owner finally talked about the seminars, the deal was ready for the wrapping paper and a bow. None of us coming from other personality preferences can follow two Merchants negotiating. As a Scientist-Hunter I would want to throttle one or both of them if I had to sit through this negotiation. But Merchants do come to an agreement. They do it in their own way, with minimal preparation, and make a decision that comes from the gut. If you are a manager, just let them do their thing and do not interrupt.

PART 2: Goals and Strategies – Where do I want to be and how do I get there?

We have now spent a lot of time preparing our starting position. You have determined whether you have an alternative source or not, who is participating in the meeting, and what your bargaining position is. Time to prepare the goals: Where you want to be. Goals clearly derive from your starting position, and especially from the strength of your bargaining position. The same holds true for the strategies and tactics you select. So, make sure you keep the right order when you prepare a negotiation: Starting Position leads to Goals, then Strategies and Tactics, in that order.

CHAPTER 12: S.M.A.R.T.+ Goals based on the Worst Case

Imagine this scenario: An architect whom I had never met before in my life called me in my office.

"I would like to speak with someone in sales," he said. "This is Bill Beauchamp with Awesome Design Group in Atlanta."

"You have him," I said. "How are you?"

We chitchatted for a few minutes. Then he mentioned the reason for his call.

"Well, I have designed a really nice mansion for a client of mine in Kiawah Island. Your company's name came up and I would like to set up a meeting," he said. Three days later I was in an airplane on the way to Atlanta.

I arrived at Awesome Design and lugged my sample case up the stairs to the second floor. The secretary asked me to wait for Bill to come down from his office.

"Hi, you must be Harry," Bill said. He was a middle-aged man with flowing grey hair wearing khakis and a shirt with a bow tie. I differentiate architects into the technical types with lots of knowledge but also very rigid in their approach, and the artists, who are happy if someone helps them translate their creative designs into a buildable project. Both, by the way, tend to fall within The Scientist personality preferences; one seeking perfection in every detail, and the other pursuing the perfect design independent of practical evaluations. Think of Frank Lloyd Wright's design of a fountain at the Florida Southern College. It took 50 years to develop the pump technology to make the dome design work, but the concept was artistic perfection.

Bill clearly seemed more the artist. He invited me into a conference room. Plans of beautiful mansions covered the walls. A side table showcased a wooden model of a house.

"Before you unpack all your stuff, let me show you what I am working on," Bill said and pointed to the model.

"Wow, this is beautiful," I admired the work. "How many square feet?"

"Just under twelve thousand," he replied.

Yes, this was a great project for us, I mused. Bill was enormously proud of his design. Over a cup of coffee, he explained the ideas and concepts of the project to me for over half an hour.

Finally, I broached the subject of cost. A house like this, on the ocean, and in a hurricane-zone would be $12 to $15 million to construct. I had done my share of houses like that. I also knew that in a hurricane zone with a requirement for impact-rated glass, windows and doors would run as high as eight to ten percent of the overall construction cost. I estimated the fenestration for this house to be anywhere from one to one and a half million dollars, depending on materials and features.

"Bill, what have you budgeted for the fenestration?" I asked.

Bill looked at me.

"The client is very cost-conscious," he began.

Right, I thought. *That's why the client is building a house in one of the most exclusive beach-front communities in the United States.*

"I was hoping to get windows and doors for about $400,000," Bill said.

What would you do in my situation? Negotiate? Not me! I hate to waste time, and in this case, I saw no chance that we would ever come to an agreement. Our numbers were just too far off from one another.

It can happen in any negotiation that goals don't overlap. I would not ever burn any bridges unnecessarily, but continuing to negotiate in a situation like this would make a conflict even more likely. So, I typically extricate myself diplomatically before frustration, disappointment, anger, and other emotions take over the conversation.

"Thank you so much for your coffee, Bill," I answered. "I hate to admit it, but we are probably not a good fit for this project. But, please, keep us in mind for any new project that comes up and where the budget is a little healthier. You really do great work and I would love to work with you in the future." Then I got up, shook hands, and turned to leave.

Now, there are two possibilities for what could happen next. One scenario is that the architect indeed has an extremely low budget and there is no chance that he can allocate over one million dollars to the windows and doors, in which case our negotiation is over for now; the budget becomes larger sometime down the road; or, the potential customer buys a cheaper window from a different vendor. If I am lucky, I will get another chance in the future.

The second possibility is that as I get up and walk towards the door, the architect jumps up.

"Wait!" he says, "don't leave just yet! Let's talk about the budget…"

What do you think my windows may now cost? One million dollars or $1.5 million? Once I recognize that the architect really wants to use my windows and doors, maybe because his customer insists, or there is no other manufacturer, he has just surrendered all his bargaining power. He had set his goals too aggressively and now has to change them in the middle of a negotiation. That is never a good idea. Let's go through proper goal-setting procedures.

Roger Fisher and William Ury coined different types of goals and the "negotiation corridor" in their influential 1981 book, *Getting to Yes*.[2] Using their work as the basis, I have a simple way to define goals. There are two distinct goals that you should prepare for each negotiation. The goal that is typically communicated during a negotiation is what I call the maximum goal. It defines the best possible outcome of the negotiation. Telling the other side what your maximum is helps define the zone of a possible agreement and moves the negotiation forward.

Bill, the architect in the earlier example, told me $400,000 was his maximum goal. The problem was that this was much too aggressive, and I couldn't see any way to come to an agreement. It was not attainable from my perspective.

The second goal you need to define is the minimum goal, which is your walk-away point. Your potential area for agreement lies somewhere between these two goals. Let me give you a scenario to consider:

---

[2] Fisher, Roger, Ury, William, Patton, Bruce, Getting to Yes: Negotiating Agreement Without Giving In (London: Penguin Group, 1981).

You are working as a buyer for the largest weaving company in Italy. The high-speed looms in your factory are set up to use polyester yarn from an American company. The supplier has its European headquarters in the UK and is one of the top yarn manufacturers in the world. Last week, you received a batch of yarn that caused a huge problem in your dyeing operation. Throughout the rolls of fabric there are streaks of yarn that dyed in a different intensity. The production has to be halted. All the warp yarn (the lengthwise strands in a woven fabric) needs to be changed out.

The supplier is fairly responsive. They send a representative to your company within a day and replace all the yarn within twenty-four hours. Still, the problem interrupted production for nearly a week. Your Sales Department is working feverishly to retain customers who are waiting for their deliveries. Manufacturing is in utter chaos. Warps with bad yarn are piled along the sides of the building. Stacks of bad fabric fill up large parts of the finished goods warehouse. The damages this quality problem has caused are in the hundreds of thousands of dollars.

Your boss comes to you a week after the factory is running smoothly again. He gives you a folder with the cost accounting of the damages. "Half-a-million dollars," he huffs. "That is the minimum I want to get from the supplier."

You call the sales representative of the supplier and organize a negotiation. He seems willing to pay something, but nothing close to a half-million dollars. You reject his offer of $50,000 outright. The meetings drag on, time flies. After three months of negotiations, the supplier makes a final offer: $498,000. Would you take it?

If you say, "Yes, why spend any more time on getting another $2,000?" then let me ask if would you take $450,000? Or

$400,000? Do you see the slippery slope of not having prepared an exact walk-away point?

If you say, "No, the boss told me $500,000 and that is my limit," then let me ask, what if it turns out that the supplier gets so agitated by this negotiation that after you reject his last offer, they cut off the deliveries? The production of fabric once again comes to a grinding halt. Only this time you lose your job.

There are two potential outcomes in this setting: You do not know when to walk away from the negotiating table and the other side can take advantage of your wavering; or, you have set the wrong point at which to walk away and lose the negotiation because the other side is in the stronger bargaining position.

So, what determines the correct minimum goal? The missing piece is what I call the worst case. Before you can determine a minimum goal, you have to think about whether or not you have an alternative. What is the worst case if the negotiation fails? And... can I accept it?

The supplier is your only option in this example. Switching yarns takes months of setup and testing. You cannot accept the worst case of the supplier not delivering yarn to your company. What should the minimum goal in this scenario be?

You must set an attainable, specific goal for your negotiation. Here, the supplier has already signaled a willingness to pay something for damages. Therefore, you should discuss the minimum goal with your boss before the negotiation. Even a refusal by the supplier to pay anything would be better than another shutdown since you cannot accept the worst case. After making sure the negotiation wouldn't collapse, you should accept the $498,000 and your boss would be delighted about the result.

Let's take this same scenario, but assume that you already have another supplier lined up. After the first quality problem, your boss has authorized setup and testing of yarn from another manufacturer. Now, as you start your negotiation, you have another supplier who can deliver immediately, at the same cost, and in perfect quality.

The worst case, namely the breakdown of negotiations, now becomes acceptable. You just bring in the other supplier. What should your minimum goal be in this case? I think your boss's goal of $500,000 is too low. Start the negotiations by asking for one million dollars. Let's see how badly the supplier wants to keep the business!

The most important consideration of setting your walk-away point is to evaluate what happens if the negotiation fails. Can you accept it? If not, be very careful with setting your minimum. Remember, changing goals in the middle of a negotiation always means losing bargaining power. In this case, it could even cost your job.

SMART + Goals

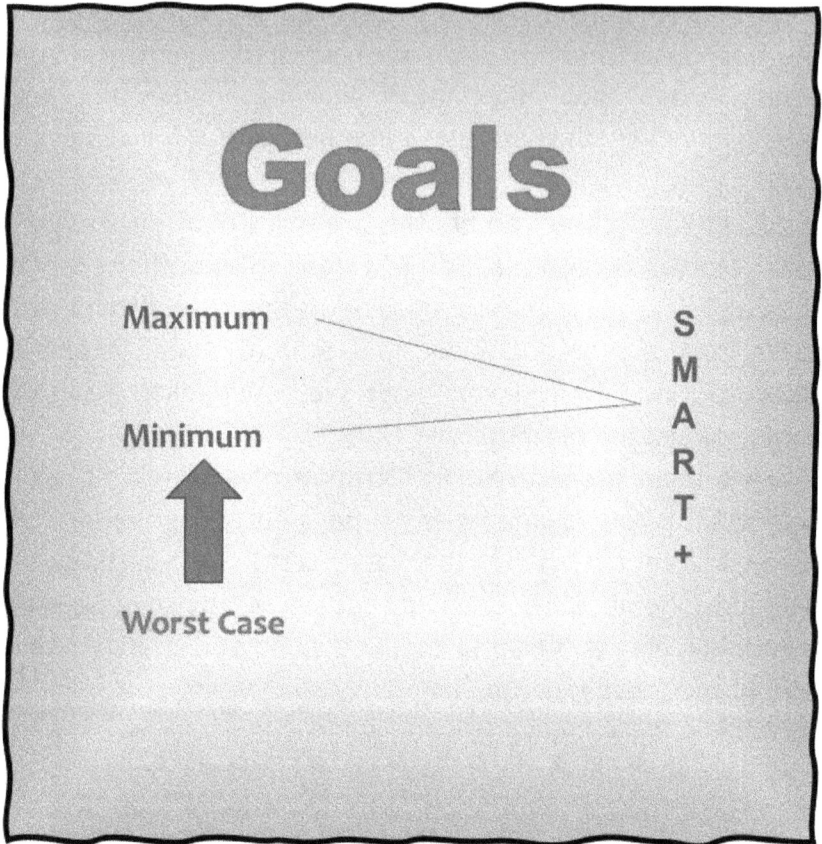

Figure 7: SMART + Goals

Management consultant George T. Doran published an article in the November 1981 issue of Management Review under the title "There's a S.M.A.R.T. Way to Write Management's Goals and Objectives."[3] Until this day, his acronym for how to set effective goals in project management processes has become the standard definition in

[3] Doran, G. T. (1981). "There's a S.M.A.R.T. Way to Write Management's Goals and Objectives", *Management Review, Vol. 70, Issue 11*, pp. 35-36.

business: S.M.A.R.T., specific, measurable, assignable, realistic, and time-related. Over the years, variations of the acronym and its meaning floated through business literature, but Doran's concept remains a clear and simple framework.

Critics of S.M.A.R.T. added two more letters to make goals S.M.A.R.T.E.R., namely 'evaluate' and 'review'. These last two attributes apply after the negotiation. I call it debriefing. I have no qualms with good debriefing manners. As a matter-of-fact, I routinely conduct post-negotiation debriefings with all my nego-tiation teams. However, in this context of preparing goals, I do not believe those two additional attributes have a place.

So, let's stick with S.M.A.R.T. for now, but let me add a new dimension to it: The plus. I found that the original Doran frame-work completely missed the psychological aspect of setting, believing in, and communicating goals. Plus stands for Psychology–the dimension of a powerful goal that transcends the obvious. It empowers your non-verbal toolset, and captures the other side's imagination, motivation, and emotion.

Have you ever been in a situation, where the other side did not believe in their own goals? Too often, management will send buyers into a negotiation with goals that are unattainable. The buyers know it. So, they don't believe in them. I have been in meetings where the buyer stated his maximum goal but imme-diately apologized for it and revised it to a lower number. The effect this has on me is the following: I just received a discount without any negotiation. That makes me wonder if there are more discounts possible. So, I hedge.

Do you see what happens? The buyer and his management in extension just gave up a lot of bargaining power. Never revise your goals in the middle of a negotiation. Over ninety percent of communication is non-verbal. Any trained negotiator will pick up on you not believing in your own goal, no matter what you say!

I will give you the standard Doran explanation for each letter, in addition to the plus, a psychological dimension, where applicable.

Specific means that you should formulate goals in a clear and precise manner. Know who should achieve them, what they entail, what has to fall in place to achieve them, and why you are pursuing them. In short, a goal should be achievable in principle. Take, for example, the lottery. I could, in theory, win the lottery.

Let me explain the psychological dimension of this goal characteristic. Your brain literally has to be able to picture the goal. Specific has a much wider ranging horizon than simply specifying what you want to achieve. Imagine a goal that specifies not smoking. What picture forms in your mind if you read this goal? None. That means this goal is not specific because you cannot picture it. You have to think about what the reason is for not smoking. Health? Sure, now you can form a picture. What do you see? I see a youthful image of myself. Someone else might see a happy face. Health or happiness are your intrinsic motivators for achieving the goal. If you can picture the goal specifically, and are motivated to reach it, then you also intuitively consider it achievable. You are priming your unconscious perception filter and enabling yourself to see something that had no specific meaning to you before. Now you notice it, and so does the other side.

Think about the goal of buying a minivan. You just had your first child and the convertible Mustang has to make way for a family coach. Your partner wants a Chrysler Town and Country with sliding doors on the driver and passenger sides. Before this moment you never had any interest in minivans. But now, driving around town, you suddenly see minivans—and especially the Chrysler your partner wants— everywhere. That is the meaning of Specific.

Motivation has both a negative and a positive dimension. If you are buying the minivan to get your partner off your back, your goal is motivated negatively. Your picture is that of you and your partner giving up the Mustang convertible and having to drive around in an ugly and boring minivan. To motivate yourself with a positive goal, your picture has to be that of your partner loving you all the more for your personal sacrifice, and your friends admiring your commitment to your new family. The new minivan now turns into a positive motivation.

Setting positively motivated, specific goals as pictures adjusts your perception filter, and, even more importantly, you also adjust the perception filter of your counterpart. Both sides are picturing this goal. Your tone of voice also changes with a clear, positively motivated picture in mind. Your voice exudes excitement, pleasure, satisfaction, and desirability. That is infectious!

Measurable adds to the specificity. A goal must be defined by a number, a percentage, or any other measurable and quantifiable metric. General terms, such as 'lower price', 'better performance', 'more efficiency', and the like are not acceptable goals. 'How much lower?' 'How much better?' 'How much more efficient?' are the questions you have to answer. Using the lottery example once more, I could, in theory, win the lottery. Winning, I define as one million dollars. Now, the goal is specific and measurable.

Here is the Plus dimension of this characteristic: If your goal is not measurable, you personally also have a hard time motivating yourself to achieve it. This lack of clarity undermines your argumentation, your body language, and your confidence. All your non-verbal communication tells the other side that you are not sure what you want.

Assignable integrates the people needed to achieve the goal. Who is on the team? Who has which role in attaining the goal? The psychological dimension of this characteristic deals with the personalities involved. Who is on my team? What motivates them? How do they act under stress? How do they make decisions?

Realistic is one of the more complicated characteristics of goals. Whether or not a goal is realistic should derive from the research. What is the market price? Do others offer the product for this price? Has your company ever sourced a product for this price? While the maximum goal should be stretching the other side to really produce significant savings, you have to make sure that the other side does not get up and walk out. The characteristic of realistic, therefore, is to a degree in the eye of the beholder. If you have done your research, you should know pretty clearly if a goal is realistic or not.

The answer to the question of realism is one of the most important, in my experience. If you set your maximum goal too high and it appears to the other side to be unrealistic, then, in the best case, you lose bargaining power and valuable time to walk your goal down to reasonable levels. The worst case is that the other side gets up and walks out. You have just ruined a perfectly good negotiation!

Think of the psychology of realism! I have to believe in my goal. I have to go into a situation of conflict and achieve a result. The perception of "realistic" is a highly subjective characteristic.

If I think that my goal is realistic, and hopefully, I did some research to test my evaluation, then I can pursue this goal in a negotiation firmly, self-assuredly, and without doubt. Any doubt of your own goals will undermine your negotiating performance.

Realistic, in the lottery example, means that winning the lottery as a goal is specific because it is statistically possible. If the goal is to win one million dollars, then it is specific and measurable. If I buy the winning ticket, it is assignable. But there is no way that I have control over winning the lottery and, therefore, the goal is unrealistic. Only if I can reach the goal and control the means to do so, is it realistic. The only way winning one million dollars in the lottery would be a realistic goal, is if I controlled the selection of the numbers.

Time-related refers to the fact that goals need to fit into schedules, deadlines, and other time-sensitive considerations. If, for example, a supplier cannot produce a part before the planned start of production of a car, the price of that part becomes irrelevant. Winning the lottery within the next fifty years would be a nice goal. But, if I need the money for a specific project next month, even eventually winning the lottery would not be a satisfactory attainment of the goal.

From a psychological perspective, this characteristic often causes grave misunderstanding. Make sure the other side understands your time considerations. On the surface, goals that have all the right characteristics but collide with time constraints more often than not cause the other side to get frustrated, aggressive, or disappointed. Imagine that the other side offered exactly what you said you wanted. Yet, you reject the offer because the timing is not right. Time considerations have to be put on the table early in the negotiation, so they won't be underestimated or ignored.

We now answered the question of where we want to be at the end of a negotiation. The last preparatory step is to figure out how to get there: Strategies and Tactics. Let's discuss these in the following chapters.

SUMMARY OF SMART

- Specific
- Measurable
- Assignable
- Realistic
- Time-related

CHAPTER 13: Going for the Kill – Pressure

Most of us who have negotiated in professional environments know how to use pressure as a strategy. It is the first thing that comes to mind, especially if we are in a position of power, like the buyer in a large corporation. Also, one particular personality type prefers pressure over all other strategies. Can you guess which one? Of course, The Hunter loves to use pressure. It is the logical consequence of looking at the world in terms of the rewards and competition it offers: How can I win, while the other side loses and the world admires my achievements?

The important message I want to convey in this chapter is that pressure is a legitimate strategy and, if properly prepared and applied, can lead to winning a negotiation. However, please pay careful attention to my word choices: Strategy implies proper preparation and intentional use. Falling into pressure because you enjoy the fight, or your emotions get in the way, or because that is all you know, or because you have not had time to prepare the negotiation, is not strategic. Applying pressure in the wrong way, or under circumstances that don't allow it, will typically lead to disaster. Bad for you. Maybe good for me, because that is when I receive a call from a client to come and help fix a negotiation that went off the rails.

Something happened to me in a negotiation that I will never forget. I was working as a key account manager for a battery manufacturer. My biggest customer was a large OEM here in the United States. We had experienced a quality problem with our battery: An explosion. Lead acid batteries contain not only sulfuric acid but also hydrogen gas. The gas develops in the chemical process of charging the battery. It is highly explosive if ignited. As a result, battery cases have an external flame arrester. A little filter allows the gas to escape and disperse harmlessly into the air, while trapping any spark before it can enter the gas-filled chamber of the battery. In this particular case, a worker at the OEM installed a battery in the trunk of a car when it exploded. Flying plastic debris and sulfuric acid caused injuries to the face of the worker. Fortunately, the cuts and burns were not serious, to all our immense relief, and the worker recovered without permanent damage within a few days.

You can imagine that all hell broke loose when this happened. The OEM threatened us with lawsuits. We tried everything in our power to mitigate the volatile situation and make sure nothing like this could ever happen again. Our Quality Department investigated the root cause of the problem, and determined that the injury was the combined result of our flawed design and mishandling of the battery. Apparently, the worker slid the battery on its plastic handles several times across the carpet of the trunk, thereby causing the case to receive a static charge. When he connected the battery to the electrical system of the car, a sudden discharge of the static electricity overwhelmed the flame arrester and caused the battery to explode.

A few weeks after this incident, the buyer for batteries at the OEM asked me to join a meeting to discuss what had happened. I knew that this was not going to be a courtesy visit with coffee and cake. I decided to bring along our vice president of quality assurance in order to be prepared for whatever was going to happen at the meeting. David was in his early sixties, ready to retire. He was calm and competent, a quintessential southern gentleman. He had also dealt with this OEM on several management levels in the past.

When we arrived at the corporate offices of the OEM, the buyer, who I knew quite well, picked us up at the reception area and took us into a meeting room. The atmosphere was tense but professional. We engaged in some superficial small talk while I awaited the big hammer. It arrived in the person of the purchasing manager about three minutes into our meeting. The door flew open.

"What is this [expletive] doing here?" the purchasing manager thundered, pointing at my companion. David froze. I looked at the manager, amazed, and wondered if I had misheard what he just said. I hadn't.

I still feel badly for David. I was the one who asked him to join me. He had never been addressed like this in his entire career of forty-some years. A southern gentleman and very much a Farmer archetype, he abhorred undiplomatic behavior and conflict in general. Then this happened. The purchasing manager had prepared the meeting with only one goal in mind: Use this unfortunate incident in the factory as leverage to reduce the price of our batteries. The only thing that stood in between me, the young, inexperienced key account manager, and a discount, was David. He knew the facts of the case, which, as I mentioned earlier, were not entirely black and white. So, the purchasing manager had obviously decided to load his gun, and literally shot my companion out of the meeting. David slumped over from the figuratively deadly injury. What did I do? Did I jump in to help my partner? No. I sat there unable to move, agape, unable to think.

David did not say another word during the entire meeting, as you can imagine. I got pummeled. Did the purchasing manager have a good strategy? Well, he got what he wanted. He also succeeded in removing from the negotiation the only person with facts and data. This definitely was a short-term win. But in the long term, there were consequences. I never trusted the buyer or his boss again. Where there had been genuine transparency and a spirit of cooperation in the past, I watched my back thereafter, never volunteered any information, and certainly made sure to prepare for all eventualities moving forward. David, who retired five years later, spent the rest of his days making my life and that of the OEM hell using passive aggressive tactics. If he found anything that could be back charged to the customer, he did not rest until it was done. When the OEM wanted to find cost savings in our production and sent teams of industrial engineers, David refused to share any data or show anything but the bare minimum to make sure those efforts failed.

Here is an absolute rule for when to use pressure: You have to be in a strong bargaining position. In our example, the purchasing manager certainly was. We had messed up, and he had leverage at that moment. There was no chance that David and I could repel the brutal attack.

If you are not in a strong bargaining position and use pressure anyway, you are counting on the other side not being prepared. You might be lucky, as so many bullies in our business are, but I would not count on it. If you meet a counterpart who is prepared and knows their bargaining position, you will lose every time!

Aside from being in a strong bargaining position, there are some more considerations. What are the consequences of using pressure? The example above illustrates that there is a danger that you could ruin an important and constructive professional relationship. If you may need the counterpart again, perhaps in a situation where you do not have all the bargaining power, you should think twice about using pressure. Too often I had the task of dealing with the aftermath of a blown-up negotiation. Once trust is broken, and personality conflict takes over the strategic task at hand, changing to a cooperative strategy is exceedingly difficult.

The story that I just shared also has an interesting ending regarding the purchasing manager. What I did not know at the time, but what I have always tried to find out since then, was that he was on his way out. He had another job lined up. So, why was he not worried about the consequences of his actions? He looked great to his bosses for the next three months—and then he was gone. The debris, the piles of broken glass left from his last negotiation remained for others to clean up.

As a manager, especially in purchasing where there is tremendous turnover, you have to make sure that your negotiators are not destroying relationships that will cost you and your company dearly after they leave. That last half percent of savings might cost a multitude more when the armies of passive-aggressive and vengeful supplier forces are unleashed. Trust me. I have had to work through negotiation situations where the level of personal conflict overrode any professional considerations.

Pressure is a win-lose strategy. Make sure, if you use it, that you can win. Also make sure that the people you are sending into battle are actually able to wield their weapons of threat, verbal abuse, arrogance, and aggression. It takes a certain personality to do what the purchasing manager in my example did. And, remember, if you are in a strong bargaining position you can use pressure, but you do not have to.

Gary Noesner, one of the founders of the modern FBI crisis negotiation training, published his account of the disastrous end to the Branch Davidian standoff near Waco, Texas in 2010.[4] In it, he borrowed a psychology term that struck me for its inherent logic in the validity of using pressure as a strategy. The 'Paradox of Power': The more we push, the more resistance we get.

So, when is pressure the right strategy to use? There are four scenarios in which I tend to use pressure:

First, a situation in which I am in a strong bargaining position, and the other side is playing an avoidance game. We will discuss avoidance strategies shortly. Trying a partnership strategy with the friendly persuasion tactic has never worked for me in that scenario.

Second, a situation in which I am in a strong bargaining position and I must have the decision-maker at the table to get my result. In that case, I purposely goad my counterpart into saying something unprofessional, maybe even offensive. Once that happens, I make a big fuss about it and refuse any further contact with the salesperson. It is a pretty rough strategy, and you certainly have to make sure that you never, ever need anything from that salesperson again. But in my experience, it works. The decision-maker comes to the table, has to apologize

---

[4] Gary Noesner, *Stalling for Time: My Life as an FBI Hostage Negotiator* (New York: Random House, 2010).

for his employee (thereby giving up bargaining power), and we can now put the finishing touches on our agreement.

Third, a situation in which I am in a weak bargaining position, but I am executing a ruse. Remember the chapter on faking an alternative? Again, there are myriad reasons not to do it, but it is a valid pressure strategy, nonetheless.

Fourth, a negotiation in which I have power but want to reach an agreement through partnership. I will briefly flash my leverage, or the consequence of a failed negotiation, with a comment such as: "The last thing I want to see is you guys losing your contract with us." Or, "I have the power to tell engineering not to test the competitor product..." (Telling, in effect, that I have the power to bring a competitor in).

Sounds like fun? Effective? Always look carefully at all your possibilities for a cooperative strategy and be mindful of the consequences before you choose a scorched earth approach.

SUMMARY OF THE PRESSURE STRATEGY:

Win-Lose Strategy
- You must be in a strong bargaining position
- The long-term effects must be acceptable
- You determine it is the best strategy to reach your goal
  - Given the starting position
  - Given the personalities involved

Tactics:
- Short or no small talk
- Uncomfortable environment (no offerings)
- Aggressive body language
- Interruption of the other side
- Undermining arguments
- Threats
- Time pressure

CHAPTER 14: Always bring a Teddy-Bear – Partnership

This chapter is about negotiating if you are in a weak bargaining position. So, let me walk you through what I call a partnership strategy. Partnership is not just a word. I have heard it too often, while at the same time my counterparts put a proverbial gun to my head. Partnership is an attitude, a true and honest willingness to find a win-win situation. Win-win also implies that, yes, both sides take something home with them, but they also give up something. Cooperative spirit involves transparency, trust, sharing of information, accepting the position of the other side, and finding a creative solution. When, in the next part of the book, we discuss the actual negotiation, you will see the ingredients for partnership: Longer small talk, good question techniques, friendly and genuine body language, and time.

My oldest son loved stuffed animals when he was four years old. All kinds of animals, some fifty years and older from his grandparents, filled up the shelves in his room. I travelled constantly at the time and tried to mitigate my sense of guilt from not being home and there for him by adding to his stuffed animal collection on a regular basis.

During one exciting weekend in rural Virginia, where we lived at the time, the county fair opened just opposite the highway on the grounds of the fire department. Not much happens in that part of the world, so, when the fair comes, the entire county congregates. Imagine the excitement and anticipation of any child driving by in a school bus on Friday afternoon, and seeing the Ferris wheel, booths, and many other rides getting set up. My son was no different. He would not rest until my wife and I agreed to take him to the fair. So, Saturday evening I had no choice but to take him. My wife stayed home with the new baby.

Music, the smell of cotton candy, and the laughter of children filled the air as we parked in front of the firehouse. The twinkling lights of the rides only added to the anticipation my son now felt.

"Papi, Papi," he said, pointing to the booth where cotton candy magically swirled on a stick, making a ball larger than the kid's head that carried it away. "Can I have some," he begged me. "Of course," I smiled, "That's why we are here."

As we walked up the hill with my son now wearing cotton candy all over his face and hair, and me on my jacket, as well, he stopped dead in his tracks.

"Look, Papi," he pointed to a booth in excitement. The booth was full of stuffed animals. They hung from the ceiling, all over the walls, but in the front of the booth sat the biggest of all—a huge teddy bear. Life-sized! That was the prize at which my son was pointing.

"I want that bear," he squealed. 'What have I gotten myself into?' I thought.

"Well, son, let's check it out," I replied, running after him up the hill. As I tried to understand what winning this teddy bear would entail, I realized that the booth had balloons filled with air on the back wall. You could buy a five-dollar ticket for three shots each with an air gun. Well, I am an accomplished hunter, so that did not sound like an insurmountable task.

I bought a ticket. As is probably often the case in these types of establishments, the gun I shot must have had a crooked barrel. I did not hit a single balloon to the great disappointment of my son! "Oh, Papi," he cried, "I really wanted to have this teddy bear." Pressure or partnership, I ask you? But I digress. Game on!

I paid another five dollars to the booth owner. This time, I knew better where to aim and shot one of the balloons. The booth owner walked up to me holding a little teddy bear attached to a key ring.

"Here, you won," he smiled. I pushed away the hand offering the little stuffed animal.

"No, Sir, I want this one," I said confidently, pointing to the life-sized prize in front of the booth.

To make a long story short, I got the bear. It took sixty-six shots and $110 dollars. Who won in this case?

You are correct, of course: first and foremost, my son won. He wanted this big teddy bear and he got it. Oh, the booth owner, you say? Yes, the booth owner also won. The teddy bear only cost $21.50 and he made more than a 500 percent profit. Anyone else? What about me? Yes, I also won. My son regarded me as "the greatest Dad in the whole wide world." Then, after figuring out how to get his prize into the rear seat of my Audi, we went home. The front door opened and my wife holding the baby appeared on the front stoop as I pulled the teddy out of the car. My son was beaming. I stood next to the bear, which was at least twice the size of my son.

"Look what we won at the fair," I called up to my wife. I never told her about the $110, of course; and she, not wanting to ruin the magic, didn't ask. I had won twice!

Why am I sharing this story? As a negotiator, you have to create this teddy bear if you are devising a win-win strategy. It has to be big, recognizable, and worth less to you than what you are getting for it. Think about it! Teddy bears are all around you. Many times, these creatures are not financial in nature. They take the form of factory tours, a supplier-of-the-year award, a special recognition from your boss, a reserved parking space... The more creative you are, the more successful your teddy bear will be.

The big Teddy Bear

Remember I mentioned in the introduction to this book how successful Porsche's Purchasing Department was, even though the carmaker was a small niche player in a much larger industry? How did they do it? I know how because I was a supplier during those years. I was lucky to meet Frieder Gamm, then a member of the Porsche purchasing team, today one of the most successful negotiation coaches and trainers in the world. We became good friends, and I am proud to have worked as a trainer and coach for Frieder Gamm Group for over a dozen years.

Our relationship did not really start in a good atmosphere. My battery company had run into trouble with the US Porsche aftermarket organization. Warranty claims for batteries were on the rise. When I investigated, I realized that most of those claims were not related to our batteries. When I refused to write a blank check and tried to negotiate with the Porsche team in the US, they threw us out and cancelled the supply contract. I was incredulous. The Hunter in me came to the fore, and, having lost the business undeservedly in my estimation, I wrote a letter to the CEO of Porsche, Dr. Wiedeking, and complained about what had happened. An investigation into the facts ensued and, as a result, Porsche reinstated us as the supplier. Rather than dealing with the organization in the US, my counterpart became Frieder Gamm in Stuttgart.

Our negotiations had always been friendly and professional. Still, Frieder remained critical of my presentation of the facts. Leading up to the eventual reinstatement of our company as a supplier, our sessions at Porsche included engineers, after-market buyers, and cost estimators. Not only had I wanted to be vindicated as a supplier, but also tried to become the supplier for the OEM batteries in addition to the US aftermarket. Frieder wanted a package deal that gave Porsche the OEM and after-market batteries for the best possible price. The negotiations were tough and lasted over several months. I really wanted this business.

Frieder took me through the factory in Stuttgart several times (teddy bear). I even got to see the holiest of all places in the factory: the room where engines were started the first time to check all functions (bigger teddy bear). Imagine the excitement of a turbo engine roaring to life! The sensation of standing next to it, hearing protection notwithstanding, and even my clothes reverberating from the vibration alone was incredible!

I could not travel to Germany on one occasion and sent my assistant instead. She went to the Weissach engineering center for an important meeting. Instead of Frieder picking her up at the reception, a man in racing suit with a helmet under his arm showed up. He asked my assistant to put on a helmet and sit in the passenger seat of a Porsche turbo rumbling in front of the door (huge teddy bear). This test driver took her on the racetrack. She later told me in jest that she thought she would not survive the experience. The car power-slid through curves at 150 mph, while the driver casually talked to her holding the steering wheel with one hand. She swore the car became airborne at one point. Afterwards, she had to negotiate with Frieder and his team. She loved fast cars, as a matter of fact, (which Frieder knew) and later said it was one of the best experiences of her life. Are you still wondering why Porsche got the best deal?

By the way, I never received the business for the OEM batteries from Porsche. Frieder and his group had a much better deal with another company. I could not touch their pricing. But Porsche reinstated my company as the sole supplier of aftermarket batteries in the United States. It was a great deal for us because we also received the right to use the Porsche logo. Was that a great teddy bear for us? Think about it. Eighty percent of our business was aftermarket retail sales. The logo of the premier sportscar in the world gave our company unprecedented recognition and added millions of dollars in sales to buying group sales like NAPA, O'Reilly, Fisher, and Alliance Auto Parts.

There are plenty more examples I could list for you, but let me conclude my Porsche stories with this one: Dr. Wiedeking, the CEO of Porsche, was a legendary leader who had brought Porsche back into prominence after a disastrous decade in the 1980s. Frieder told me the story of a tough supplier with whom he once had to negotiate.

"It went really well, after he shook hands with Dr. Wiedeking," he smiled at me when we began to discuss the case.

He shook hands with Dr. Wiedeking? A low-ranking supplier and the CEO of Porsche? Yes, this actually happened. Frieder and his counterpart had lunch in what is still today probably the nicest cafeteria of any company I have seen. Suddenly, a murmur rippled through the room, as Dr. Wiedeking came to get lunch for himself. He made a point of eating where his employees ate. On the way to the buffet, he stopped at the table where Frieder and his counterpart were sitting. The two men scrambled up from their seats.

"You must be Herr Ohnesorg from Bosch," Dr. Wiedeking said.

The man nodded and shook the CEO's hand.

"Nice to meet you. Give my best to Dr. Schmidt [the head of Sales]," Wiedeking continued, "Mr. Gamm here will take good care of you. I hope you will come up with a good solution for us."

He smiled and walked away. How hard, do you think, the Bosch salesman would negotiate after this chance encounter. Not only had the CEO of Porsche acknowledged his existence, but he even knew his name, which shows appreciation, interest, and respect. Furthermore, he gave the impression of personally watching over the result of the ongoing negotiation. Who would want to screw that up?

Wait a minute! How did Dr. Wiedeking know the salesman's name? Frieder smiled. If you had a difficult negotiation on the calendar, Dr. Wiedeking allowed buyers to consult his secretary. If he was in town that day, he would come to the table the buyer had specified and greet the supplier by the name the buyer had previously submitted. The entire encounter had been planned minutely. And, yes, it was a great teddy bear. It cost two minutes of Dr. Wiedeking's valuable time that likely resulted in millions of dollars of savings.

My predecessor in the battery company I ran in the mid-1990s told me about another great teddy bear. At that time, BMW had built its factory in Greer, South Carolina. Rudy, my predecessor, was in charge of supplying batteries from North Carolina to the new factory with just-in-time deliveries. That meant that the correct battery had to be on the line and fully charged at the exact time the car for which it was intended came through. The suppliers had full responsibility for this just-in-time delivery system. My boss always compared batteries to vegetables because they discharge while in storage and have to be recharged after a fairly short time. It was a logistical challenge to always have fully charged batteries on the production line, in different sizes and specifications for different cars. It did not always work smoothly as you can imagine. My predecessor and BMW had their share of problems and a tough back-and-forth, especially during the startup period.

Rudy's office received a call one Monday morning from the BMW Purchasing Department.

"We need you to come here to the factory on Thursday at 9:00 am," was the cryptic message, "and tell Rudy he needs to bring a 70 AH (Ampere Hour) battery with him."

When the secretary inquired about the reason for the visit, the answer was vague. "He will find out when he gets here."

You can imagine that Rudy was quite nervous about this request. What could be the reason? Was there another quality problem? Why bring a battery? All these questions swirled in his head as he contemplated what to do.

The first decision he made was to build a battery in the lab. He wanted to make sure that the battery he carried to the meeting was guaranteed perfect in terms of quality and appearance. So, he called the engineer responsible for the BMW business and they hand built a perfect battery the next day.

Rudy registered with the receptionist at the BMW facility in Greer at the appointed time. He expected someone from the Purchasing Department to pick him up. Instead, a man in a dark suit shook his hand and handed him a business card: Legal Department. Now, Rudy really got nervous. Why would someone from the Legal Department need to meet with him? This did not bode well.

The two men went into a small meeting room adjacent to the main hall of the BMW plant. The lawyer opened his briefcase and extracted a pile of papers.

"Sign these," he motioned to Rudy.

"I guess I need some time to read them," he replied.

"Not much time. Hurry up!" The lawyer said.

Rudy looked at the documents. They were longwinded nondisclosure agreements. So, he quickly signed them. They left the meeting room, and the lawyer handed Rudy over to a lady with a white lab coat who was waiting for him at the reception desk.

She led him through some dark hallways into a room requiring finger scans and high security clearance to enter. After they entered the room, Rudy adjusted his eyes to bright lights. A Z3 BMW, the car that BMW wanted to introduce within the next twelve months was parked in the middle of the room. A group of technicians, engineers, people with charts and notebooks swarmed around the brightly lit, sleek metallic-blue convertible with a tan interior.

It was the James Bond car for *Golden Eye*, the next movie of the franchise that BMW sponsored at the time. The engineers allowed Rudy to ceremoniously fit 'his' battery into the car.

Can you imagine? What an incredible display of team spirit and trust BMW showed their supplier! How much did it cost? Nothing. As a matter of fact, BMW received a mint battery free of charge. What did this do to the relationship with our battery company? Rudy now felt as if he were one of 'them'. He now had a personal stake in the success of BMW and would do anything in his power to make that happen. That's the power of a teddy bear!

Just a year later, Rudy retired, and I took over the business. It did not take long for BMW to beguile me into their seductive web of partnership. My eyes still well up when I think wistfully of my days working with BMW. I saw electric car prototypes twenty years before their time, we socialized in fully sponsored annual national dealer meetings, I got to know the BMW plants in Bavaria, South Carolina, and Johannesburg well. We were part of a team. And, yes, we had tough negotiations with millions of dollars at stake, but as a supplier, I focused my efforts on making my customer happy and profitable. After all, they made me feel that I had a stake in their success—and I still believe I did.

Needless to mention that I drive a BMW today, twenty-some years after having been a supplier.

Think foremost about the advantages of partnership as a negotiation strategy! You can count on long-lasting relationships with your customers or suppliers. You have a much greater chance of getting the best deal up front as a buyer. You establish trust and transparency and receive the same in return. And, when you are in a bind, you can count on the other side to be willing to help. Thinking that way is not a weakness. It is pure strength!

In my training seminars I use a specific case for the participants to prepare and negotiate. The case is fairly simple: You, the OEM buyer, switched suppliers for large cost savings. It turns out that the cost savings resulted in huge quality problems with the new supplier. Your task after only six months is to bring back the old supplier—at any cost!

What would you do? Most of the teams of buyers correctly choose partnership as their strategy, but never let the old supplier know why they are calling him back. The result is almost consistently that the two teams cannot agree on terms and fail to sign an agreement.

Why? Where is the trust and transparency in this case? Imagine a real situation in which you made a grave mistake. You have personally known your counterpart for many years. How about apologize, stitch together a nice teddy bear, and appeal to their humanity? Anybody can make a mistake. Buying teams in my trainings rarely choose this bare-it-all approach. But when they do, they always get a good result. It seems that we have forgotten how to say "please", "thank you", and "I am sorry." Remember, partnership is an attitude, not a platitude!

Now that we loaded up on stories and examples, let's discuss some of the down-to-earth tactics that support a partnership strategy. Location certainly is an important one. Remember The Farmer, the personality that strives for harmony and safety. If you determine that your counterpart has this personality preference, consider negotiating at their location. Show respect, take a plant tour, and admire the new machines rather than criticizing the amount of waste. Bring something with you, like a jacket for the salesperson with the logo of your company stitched on it. Remember, Farmers identify with a team.

If you cannot negotiate at the supplier's location, still make sure that your meeting room is large enough, has good lighting, that the heating and air conditioning work, and is quiet, so that you and your counterpart can fully concentrate. I know that some of my bigger customers have rules that suppliers cannot be offered anything. Not a good idea! Remember, in a partnership strategy you want the other side to be relaxed and open to finding that great win-win solution with you. A grumbling stomach, no water in a meeting lasting for hours, no coffee in the morning, and no lunch during lunchtime are all working against you. A cup of coffee is a small price to pay for a counterpart's willingness to cooperate with you, potentially saving millions of dollars. Also, don't overwhelm the other side with additional negotiators, the old three-against-one routine, that puts the other side on the defensive.

Think of the timing for your negotiation. Nothing is worse than creating unnecessary time pressure. Allow for plenty of breaks for both sides to keep their heads cool. Think about how far your counterpart has to travel to come to the meeting. One buyer that I encountered as a salesman always set meetings at

8:00 AM in the morning. I had to get up at 5:00 AM to be there on time. The buyer was not even there on many occasions, and instead showed up thirty minutes late. If she was pursuing a pressure strategy, these are valid tactics. But she was not. She just did not think about what her scheduling meant to me. Her being late sent me over the edge, especially since I grew up in a very punctual culture. I inferred that she did not respect me, rather seemingly enjoyed mistreating a low-ranking, young salesman. I did not like her, and that made me less cooperative.

There is only one personality type that enjoys a fight: The Hunter. There are few applications for successfully using pressure, as you have read in this chapter on partnership strategies. The Hunters among us have to work especially hard on preparing partnership strategies and tactics. There are very few negotiations, especially with regard to personality preferences, in which a pressure strategy lets you achieve your goals better than with partnership. No personality other than the Hunter works well when attacked. Scientists become stubborn, Farmers get passive aggressive, and Merchants deflect and duck. I see pressure used way too often in my experience, and rarely successfully. Why? Either negotiators never learned another strategy in the pressure-based corporate culture that formed them, or they did not prepare well.

Partnership takes more time to develop, both in preparation and execution. It also leaves more options, including the possibility that if the cooperative approach is not netting the desired results, the negotiation can swing to a pressure strategy. Going the other way around, from a failed pressure strategy to partnership approach, is difficult. It will involve replacing negotiators to eliminate personality conflict, somehow repairing the trust deficit, and spending a lot of extra time on preparing the right teddy bear to make the abrupt reversal of strategy digestible.

There are lots of Teddy Bears around you! Just look for them!

Win-Win Strategy
- Typically used in a weaker bargaining position
- Or when a relationship is sought or needs to be maintained
- Always have a "Teddy Bear" prepared
- You determine it is the best strategy to reach your goal
  - Given the starting position
  - Given the personalities involved

Tactics:
- Extensive small talk
- Comfortable and familiar environment
- Transparency (share information)
- Cooperation (friendly body language)
- Establish trust
- Show interest in the other side

Chapter 15: Stalling for Time – Avoidance and Acceptance

While pressure and partnership are the main negotiation strategies among which to choose, there are two secondary strategies to consider, as well. You can either try to buy time (avoidance) or you settle a negotiation to create an advantage for another future negotiation (acceptance). Neither strategy really wins the negotiation on its own. You will still move into a pressure or partnership approach to conclude an agreement.

Let me explain an actual situation, in which this made all the difference. A new invention rattled the marketplace while I worked in the battery industry. Up to that time, we manufactured the lead plates that make up the individual cells in a lead-acid battery on casting machines. It was a process that basically had not changed since Thomas Edison's time. Then, a new technology arrived from metal fence production: An expanded metal grid. This technology cut slots into a bar of lead. A machine then pulled the bar apart and created an expanded metal grid. This new way of manufacturing plates created several huge advantages. Though the expanded metal plates had the same surface area as their casted counterparts, they were up to one third lighter. That was a huge advantage that affected both price and weight of the battery.

Imagine that you bought batteries from a company with the traditional casting technology. You had maybe three approved companies from which to source your batteries. Suddenly, you hear from Engineering that they have been working with one of these companies on approving a new battery made with expanded metal technology. The testing, you found out, would be concluded in three months. Let us assume that you had three months' time to decide. Clearly, you would wait to conduct your negotiation until you had this alternative, a cheaper technology and a lighter battery favored in your Engineering Department.

Avoidance as a negotiation strategy only works under one scenario: You find yourself in a weak bargaining position that, over an acceptable time, will improve. Do not, I repeat emphatically, do not use avoidance if your bargaining position does not improve in the future or, even worse, when you do not have the time to wait for the alternative to become real. Pushing claims and uncomfortable negotiations ahead of you so that, hopefully, your successor has to deal with it, is not strategic. As we saw in the previous chapter on claims, avoidance in such a case can ruin a potentially good negotiation.

What are some of the tactics best suited for avoidance? I am sure you might have a few ideas, such as vacation, sickness, too much work, a broken computer... My number one approach is always to blame a higher power that is not in the room: The engineers are not done with their drawings; my boss has me working on something else; the Quality Department is not signing off on the new factory; the Finance Department is dragging its feet... You get the drift.

Time is also a factor when you might decide to use acceptance as a strategy. Although acceptance is not really a negotiation strategy in itself, there are situations when accepting an offer from the other side rather than negotiating might be better. Accepting the offer from the other side often is a result of running out of time. I have recommended settling a claim with the supplier in several cases I have coached for the sake of being able to start with the important negotiation on a clean slate. Think of situations in which you knew of potentially embarrassing facts, a risk factor that, once out in the open, could ruin your negotiation. For example, you may, for whatever reason, not have purchased the number of parts specified as a prerequisite for a volume discount. Yet, your company took the discount anyway. How about just extending the contract without much discussion, especially if volumes continue to decline?

You may have experienced the other side using avoidance against you. Frustrating? Infuriating? You feel slighted? Do not! Either your counterparts are not tactical in their selection of strategy, and are bad negotiators, or they are working through a real or perceived problem with their bargaining power. As you are preparing your negotiation and determining your bargaining power, you should find out why the other side believes it is in a weak bargaining position, and what they are waiting for that will improve it.

Breaking the avoidance strategy of the other side is important for you. Your leverage is the weakness that the other side perceives of itself. Use it! In my experience, avoidance usually requires pressure to resolve. Think about a good guy-bad guy scenario. Maybe your boss swinging the proverbial baseball bat would be an acceptable tactic to shake things loose. Once you get the other side to the table before their delay bears fruit, you have a great chance to win your negotiation. I am typically happy when I sense avoidance. The power is on my side, even if the weakness on the other side might only be perception and not reality.

Delay Strategy
- Typically used in a weaker bargaining position but gets stronger over acceptable time
- You determine it is the best strategy to reach your goal
  - Given the starting position
  - Given the personalities involved

Tactics:
- Blame a higher power
- Find excuses for inaction
- Create barriers in moving forward

PART 3: Execution

Here we are, ready to negotiate. We are well prepared, we think we know who is coming, what bargaining power our counterparts may have, what goals they might be pursuing, and how they might go about it. Time to execute! Wait! We don't know if our preparation and interpretation of what we know are correct. Certainly, we can never be sure if our preparation is 100% accurate. I always try to surprise the other side in the negotiations I conduct, so that I can pull them onto my turf, into my strategy, and towards my goals.

How do we verify that we are on the right track? That is what this part is all about: How to use great techniques in verbal and non-verbal communication, psychology, and observation. We need to learn to observe, observe, and observe some more. If you had to take a wild guess, how much communication is verbal versus non-verbal? Fifty percent, sixty percent, maybe even eighty percent? According to Professor Albert Mehrabian, the guru of non-verbal communication research, the correct answer is that 93% of all communication is non-verbal. That includes 55% body language, and 38% tone of voice.

The topics I selected for this partition of your toolbox are stress management, question techniques, communication strategies, body language, and lie detection. These are the tools that will get you across the finish line.

CHAPTER 16: Just Leave the Light On

Imagine you are walking down a path in the jungle of Sumatra. This is the only place in the world where tigers, rhinos, orangutans, and elephants live together in the wild. Since you are by yourself, you are nervous. There are lots of noises in the jungle. Suddenly, you hear rustling leaves behind you. As you turn around to look, you see a Sunda tiger jump out onto the path and run towards you.

You stare at it and you wonder whether the animal might be hostile or not... No way! If you did that, you would certainly be killed. Mother Nature has actually programmed our brains to assist in a situation like this. Rather than losing precious time analyzing the life-threatening situation, the thinking part of your brain shuts down completely, meaning that all synapses connecting the different areas of the brain with your nervous system in your body disconnect. The non-conscious part of your brain, the autonomous nervous system that usually regulates heart rate, respiration, digestion, and sexual arousal takes over. You now only have access to one of three possible emergency programs available for immediate use: Fight, flight, or play dead.

Why a person chooses one over the other is a huge topic in neuroscience and behavioral sciences. Depending on the stress level and on how much of your brain has shut down, certain personality preference types choose flight over fight. You guessed right: The conflict-shy personalities like The Farmer and The Scientist are more likely to choose flight, while The Hunter prefers the fight. However, it is much more complicated than this. If there is a way out of a life-threatening situation, most people tend to choose flight. People who are cornered tend to fight. The third emergency program, to play dead, only occurs in situations when the fight or flight mechanism has failed. Playing dead is our last defense.

Let's go back to the tiger in the jungle. You don't pause and ponder whether the tiger might hurt you or not. Most likely, you will run as fast as you can, especially if you have no weapon. And that is a point of interest. You will be able to run faster than you have ever run before. Why? Thanks to your emergency programming, your adrenal system outfits you with chemicals that create superhuman strength. A cocktail of hormones, adrenocorticotropic, epinephrine, and cortisol flood the body. They message the liver to produce glucose, and the muscles to turn all available fat into immediate energy. A hefty dose of adrenaline increases blood pressure and breathing to prepare the muscles for utmost exertion. You now can run as you never have before. If you have a weapon or your survival instinct tells you to fight, you have access to the same superhuman strength.

Does that sound like a great experience? Not really. The heart of the issue is still the fact that you might die. What does this have to do with negotiations? Let me take your pulse and make you think about the last time you attended a negotiation. You got really mad. Remember? You may not even remember exactly what happened at the end or what was said. All you could think about was getting the hell out of the room. Maybe you did not want to run. Maybe you felt your neck swell, your fists clench, and all you could do was fight the impulse to lunge across the table at your counterpart. Thankfully, the last few synapses remained connected. Otherwise, you would be reading another book right now called, "How do I find a new job?"

I want you to remember that moment when you became really frustrated. Think of the first physical change that happened to you. We all have similar symptoms when stress takes over, but perhaps not the same at the onset. Most people will feel the rising blood pressure. The ears start burning, the neck swelling, or the face blushing. Others will notice their muscles tensing, the famous pencil-cracking-in-half moment, or the sweaty palms. Yet others first feel sick to their stomach, get tunnel vision, lose hearing, or feel tingling in strange places from all available blood flowing into muscles. All these symptoms have to do with your body preparing to deal with the emergency at hand.

Remember to notice your personal first symptom, and be conscious of what it means: You are getting stressed. The next thing that will happen to you is that your pre-frontal cortex, the part of your brain that governs reasoning and verbal communication, shuts down. Since we rarely deal with bloodthirsty tigers in a negotiation (although I have been physically threatened a time or two), the disconnect of our synapses happens slower than when the tiger is running after us. The light in the thinking brain goes out, bulb after bulb, until it gets completely dark.

Once more, think back to the last time you experienced a great amount of stress. I have sat in meetings during which I suddenly could not remember anything to say. I was well prepared but... all gone. Even worse, as a foreign speaker, I tend to lose my vocabulary under high stress. Although I have lived in the US for over thirty years now and have written several books in English, I suddenly cannot remember English vocabulary. A German word comes to mind. What is going on? The synapses to my speech center have disconnected. Some people stutter for the same reason.

Remember the meeting with your boss, when you sat there being pummeled and could not think of one thing to say in defense? But later that afternoon in the car on the way home, you slap your forehead because the perfect answer comes to mind. "I should have said..." What is happening? Your synapses are slowly reconnecting, just an hour or so too late.

This brings me to the management part of stress management: How do I prevent this from happening? I described some instances of identifying the first physical symptoms of stress. If you can recognize them, chances are that you are still fairly well connected. Most of the lights are still on upstairs. You consciously recognize that, oops, emotions are taking over. You are aware of becoming agitated, frustrated, angry, or disappointed. That is the best moment for intervention. Stop the process of synapses disconnecting. The example in which you suddenly remember what you should have said to your boss, an hour too late in the car on the way home, illustrates what you need: You need to buy time!

Time in a negotiation is hard to come by. Usually, as we are in the middle of the battle, there is no time. We push on, try to get through the tough spot. The harder we try, the more likely it will be that we become stressed. We forget our preparation as the stress builds. We also lose the ability to observe the other side and register nonverbal signals, and we are unable to make strategic decisions.

How do we buy time? Here are some basic tools to remember: Rule #1: TAKE A BREAK! If you are feeling stressed, the best thing you can do is to take a break. Invite the counterpart to go with you and get a coffee. Ask for a water break. A bathroom break usually is an acceptable excuse, as well. I prepare breaks when I expect to be in a tough negotiation. I used to tell my secretary to interrupt the meeting if she heard loud voices. She would open the door and notify me that "Germany was on the line." 'All of it?' I wondered. I would then excuse myself, walk out of the conference room and take a handful of deep breaths while relaxing my shoulders and leg muscles.

Rule #2: TAKE A BREAK! If you feel that you can't leave the meeting, take a mental break. Purposely slow down your conversation. Throw the ball into the other court with a well-placed open question. Or have your counterpart repeat their question. Take ten seconds to respond. Yes, you Hunters out there, no one ever gets penalized for not answering right away. Control your breathing. Concentrate on it. Lower your voice. Purposely work on being calm and collected. There you go, do you feel how things are slowing down? How the adrenaline slowly dissipates? How the fog lifts and mental clarity returns? Aaah.

Rule #3: TAKE A BREAK! There is another important technique that I always use for difficult negotiations. I never go into a meeting by myself when a lot is at stake. Bring someone with you. Only one person talks (most of the time), which means that your partner is there to observe and stay fully connected. If you get stressed, your partner can take over while you concentrate on your breathing. Who do I select to join me? Well, I am a Hunter type, so which personality can assist me best with sensing conflict and negotiating it? You are right: The Merchant. A Merchant will always be the first to sense conflict and try to mitigate it, because that personality thrives on contact and relationship.

Rule #4: TAKE A BREAK! Get yourself in a calm and collected demeanor before the negotiation. Through my work as an author and historian, I have given speeches and presentations to large audiences. Imagine the situation: Students and their professors assemble in a large auditorium at a university to hear me speak for an hour. I am behind stage, wired with a microphone, and holding a clicker in my hand to run the slide presentation on the three large screens behind the podium. I have fifteen minutes before showtime. Generally, I don't work from notes and I despise lecterns. I want to see, feel, and work with my audiences.

So, I usually sit somewhere off to the side, and in my mind go over the presentation, the anecdotes, and the moments when certain photographs or graphics have to pop up behind me. This is also the time when I concentrate on nothing else but myself, my breathing, and my heartbeat. I always manage to stay calm, and not be nervous. I know that no one out there knows more about my topic than me. My books are the result of decades of archival study and analysis. There is no reason to be nervous about my knowledge. It is all about the stagecraft now. Can I be interesting? Entertaining? Confident? Speak clearly? Have the right posture? Then, I hear the moderator announce me. The audience claps in anticipation, and out I come. Now it is showtime and I am ready.

The worst thing that can happen to me in such a moment is that some stagehand disturbs me backstage, fumbles around with my microphone or sending unit, or mumbles something about the screen projector not working. Suddenly, I am ripped out of my state of concentration, and I take on the nervousness of the stagehand. Then, I can guarantee that my performance will not be as smooth as it could and should be.

Why am I telling you this? Being ready to negotiate is about entering the conference room with a low stress level. It is not helpful for most people to cram information an hour before the negotiation. Keep stress away from you. Prepare well, because that increases your confidence and decreases your fear (i.e. stress) that the other side has something on you that you may not have thought about. Get to work early. Don't risk the stress of being stuck in traffic and worrying you might not make it to the meeting on time. Don't take phone calls or read e-mails just before the meeting. Try to keep personal problems, like an angry partner or sick kids, away from your task at hand. Find a quiet place to sit down, review your notes, and focus on your breathing and pulse. If you have a partner in your negotiation, involve them in the quiet time. Then, walk onto the negotiation stage, confident, calm, and aware.

We all have to work on staying fully connected. None of the tools I am showing you for executing a negotiation work without having the light on upstairs. The Hunters among us have the steepest learning curve, but once we conquer our short temper, impatience, and proud ego, we will be equipped to win. Hunters, by the way, are also the personalities who will use pressure as a strategy, and purposely push the other side into losing their calm. It is a form of bullying in the extreme. Don't be bullied. Deescalate, stay calm, use your preparation, and you can easily diffuse any such onslaught. Partnership requires both sides to be fully connected so they can find that sweet spot of a win-win agreement.

Chapter 17: Will You Take Me to Dinner Tonight?

Why ask questions? To get information? Sure. What about other purposes? Can you use questions to set the atmosphere of a meeting? Short, closed-ended questions certainly can convey your intention of using a pressure strategy. To clarify? You bet. I have often been the dumb guy in the meeting who raised his hand. "I don't get it. Can you explain this to me again?" Then, looking around the table, I would see a lot of relieved faces. They didn't get it either. How about showing interest in the other side through questions? Do you have children? How long have you lived here? What do you miss most about your home state? These questions are usually open-ended and give the other side a chance to convey their information. Can you manipulate the counterpart through question techniques? Yes, you can, and I will show you some examples momentarily.

Asking good questions is essential for a negotiation in which you are the underdog. You need to find out what the other side is bringing to the table. How willing are they to make a deal? What kind of attitude are they bringing with them? Can you confirm your preparation about their goals, their strategies, their motivations, and their personalities? This chapter examines two perspectives: How to defend yourself against manipulation; and, how to acquire great questioning skills.

Lots of question techniques are manipulative. I want to introduce some of those questions to help you guard against them. Of course, you can also study those techniques and use them in a negotiation.

As a big proponent of trust, transparency, and cooperative negotiation strategies, I rarely use overtly manipulative questions. Therefore, I will also introduce you to basic question techniques that are easy to use. They are designed to find out what you need to know without overtly manipulating the other side.

QUESTION CHAINS

I play the following game with participants in my trainings. I ask one of the people in the room to take me to dinner. I do this in the first of a suite of modules, so the participants usually have never met me before.

I focus on one participant and ask out of the blue.

"Will you take me to dinner tonight?"

What answer am I expecting? They do not know me and have no reason to invite me to dinner. The negative response usually comes quickly. (Believe it or not, this never works in Sweden or Latin America, where people are just too friendly to say "no", even if they have no plans whatsoever to ever take you to dinner.) I feign disappointment. Then I ask everyone, especially my target, to forget that I asked the question.

Now, I ask them for permission to get some information. Their body language betrays that they are a little nervous, looking at me wide-eyed while wringing their hands, wondering what comes next. The conversation goes something like this:

"So, I gather that you are working for the Purchasing Department. What is your responsibility?"

"I purchase metals."

"Fascinating! Wow! So, the steel tariffs must really be giving you a fit?"

"Yes, it's tough right now."

"It seems like you are doing a great job given this situation. How many parts are you sourcing?"

"About two dozen."

"Two dozen? That sounds like a lot of work. Are they all from different suppliers?"

"No, not all. I have about five different suppliers." I am watching how she becomes more comfortable with this line of questioning. After all, she knows all the answers, and so far, none of the questions are personal. This is easy.

"Five suppliers. Do you like any of the salespeople?"

"Not really. They work for big companies. We are usually not their biggest customer. They get pushy sometimes."

"That sounds tough. You must be negotiating against the odds often. Has volume been increasing or decreasing lately?"

"Decreasing. That makes my job even harder. Prices are rising while our purchasing volume is decreasing."

"You are getting squeezed from both sides. So, how often are you negotiating?"

"You mean in a week?"

"Yes, in a week."

"Four to five times."

"That's a lot. You must feel a lot of pressure. Do you have enough time to prepare these negotiations?"

"Never. I'm always in a rush."

"Ouch. You seem so collected and on top of it while telling me this. Do you always reach your goals when you negotiate?"

"Not always. But I still have my job, you know."

"You must be really good. When you say, 'not always,' what percentage of times do you reach your goals?"

"Half the time, probably. I get close about three quarters of the time."

"I am blown away! Especially in that industry! Would you like to reach your goals every time?"

She sits up. Her interest is palpable.

"Well, yes. Who wouldn't?"

"Exactly. I think, I have brought something with me that you may find interesting. I am working on a research project with Michigan State University. We have been working on a software package for three years—just for buyers. It will help you reach your goals. In fact, we are pretty close to releasing it, and the marketing plan includes that we will guarantee that, if you use our program, you will always reach your goals."

"Really? But how does that work? How does the program make this possible? It sounds unrealistic."

"Well, I have tested most parts of it, and if you use it correctly it works. The professor, a really famous guy in his field, has issued a beta version of the package and we who work on the project are supposed to find people willing to test the software. You would be perfect for this!"

"You think?"

"I do. Let me propose this to you: You take me to dinner tonight and I can show you the software." I point to my laptop. "I have it right here."

It is a game of probability for me, as you can imagine, but I am always surprised how many times I actually get a 'yes'. Granted, a time or two, it might be a gesture of good will to help me out with my seminar. Many times, though, my counterparts literally have forgotten the initial question, where I stated my goal, "Will you take me to dinner tonight?" Instead, they're ensnared in my questioning. I hope that all of you will agree that, at a minimum, my chances of getting a 'yes' have dramatically improved between the first, blunt question and the second, following a careful leading-up to the main question.

This is a technique called Question Chains. Every salesperson has heard of it. Most sales trainings include the use of question chains, usually a significant part of product training for sales forces. No, it is not about the product. It is about the need. Can I persuade the other side to describe a need that I actually defined, to then allow me to fit my product snuggly into that need? That is the manipulation. And it works. Some companies built their entire revenue on door-to-door sales. Ever heard of Kirby vacuums? Avon? Sellers of Bibles, reference books, and software? These sound like dinosaurs in 2020. Well, they are still thriving all across rural neighborhoods in this country. Companies such as AT&T and SBC Communications knock on doors in those same neighborhoods and talk people into switching carriers. Just like that. If you think direct sales are fading, think about the tool truck sitting in front of a repair shop, or the frozen food delivery truck in suburban neighborhoods. Last year, direct selling in the United States accounted for almost $29 billion. Companies relying on that sales channel spend a lot of money on psychologists to create question chains for their door-to-door sales forces.

Many years ago, I played in a rock band as a drummer. I really enjoyed it. We had recorded a CD with all original songs, and played regionally in clubs and small open-air venues with some level of success. The gigs were tough. A performance day usually started in the late morning. We loaded our PA system, amps, instruments, lighting equipment, and seemingly thousands of cables into our trailer. Then, we drove to the town and locale where we were playing, usually an hour or two from our studio. Unpacking and setting up the stage took three or four hours. Then, we had to check that everything worked, which it usually didn't. We scrambled to find the problem, change out the connector, fuse, cable, amplifier, or whatever malfunctioned to get the system to run. By now it was about 6:00 PM, time for a drink and something to eat.

The show usually started with our warm-up band at 8:00 PM, and we would start playing around 9:30 PM until 12:00 AM or, when the crowd was good, even longer. While everybody left or closed out the evening at the bar, we broke down the stage, carefully packaged everything exactly where it needed to be, and loaded the trailer to head home. We finally would go to sleep around 3:00 or 4:00 AM. The money was negligible. Since I managed the band, I got to fight with the club owners to get paid what they had promised. I also had to collect the door money which, when we had our own doormen, was easy. We were usually ripped off when the club refused to let our guy collect the cover charge. Once I received the money we were due, I paid our sound technician, the warm-up band, deduct the gas money, add the CD sales of the night, and split the rest with my bandmates. We were lucky if we made $150 per person for sixteen to seventeen hours of work.

So, we obviously didn't do it for the money. We did it because we loved it and there is no better way to study teamwork than with a group of people who have no other material incentive to work together. We all had jobs to subsidize the meager artist income we generated. Only one of my bandmates, a brilliant guitarist, cartoon artist, and definitely from the Flower Power generation, had trouble finding and holding jobs. He refused to work in the area in which he had the most skills, like playing guitar as a studio musician, or illustrating for a publisher as he was a gifted cartoonist. Jason could play solos off the cuff that sounded exactly like Carlos Santana would have played them, or Mark Knopfler, or David Gilmour. Working as a studio musician, and playing what others wanted him to play, in his opinion, diminished the art and, therefore, would be an unacceptable compromise.

He usually worked as a driver for some van company, which was helpful in his work with us because he could drive to rural Virginia from Washington D.C. with a paid car. More often than not, however, he did not have one of those part-time jobs. Then, he was hard-up for money.

One day, during a practice session, Jason burst in, exuberant.

"I found a new job!" he exclaimed. We all stared at him, agape with surprise.

"That's great!" we oohed and aahed in chorus. "What is it?"

"I am selling coupon books for paintball outings!" Jason beamed.

We all looked to the floor. 'Well, that's not going to last,' I could all but hear my bandmates thinking. Jason, while being a gifted lead guitarist and one of the nicest people you could ever wish to meet, was a total introvert. I could not imagine him working in a sales job that required him to be outgoing. Had I not been to his house, I would never have seen the volumes of illustrations he made of kids' fairy tales. He never even attempted to sell his work nor make any use of it other than to perfect his craft. He was a Scientist par excellence. He even refused to move into the spotlight when laying down a brilliant guitar solo during our performances. Jason stayed in the background, sometimes playing with his back to the audience, and hardly ever addressed, or even acknowledged the crowd.

I must admit that I shared the pessimism of my bandmates about Jason's prospects for success in his new job. Jason's territory to sell these coupon books was K Street in Washington D.C., I later found out. Anyone know K Street? That is where the most prestigious law firms and lobbying outfits have their offices. High end! Picture marble foyers, a receptionist intercepting traffic to the back offices, lawyers charging upwards of $500 per hour. That was Jason's territory.

I kept asking about how his new job was going when we met for band practices and performances.

"Great," Jason would say. He missed one weekend performance because the company that had hired him took all the new salespeople on a retreat somewhere in West Virginia. The week after he returned, I asked about the retreat.

"How was it?" I asked.

"Oh, great," Jason responded. Typical of a Scientist, I had to pull information out of him with brute force.

"What did you do?" I kept up my line of questioning.

"We practiced how to sell the coupon books," he smiled smugly.

"Well, how are you doing it?" I was starting to get frustrated.

"Here, I can show you," Jason finally volunteered. He went outside to his car and came back with a three-ring binder.

"It's all in here," he said, signaling that the conversation had ended.

So, I started reading. It was a manual with question chains. They were professionally conceived, using mirroring, labeling (see later in the next chapter), and other psychological means to engage and influence the other side. Clearly, a psychologist had had a hand in drafting these questions.

The sales process consisted of individual barriers. Barrier #1 was the receptionist; barrier #2, the secretary in the law office; barrier #3, the actual lawyer or lobbyist.

The questions read, "If you meet the receptionist, smile, complement them on something personal like their dress or their hair, then ask…", "If the answer is yes, follow up with this question…", "If the answer is no, ask this question…", and on and on it went. The goal was to get through each barrier and end up with the largest possible group, like four lawyers and their aids who would then, supposedly, buy the coupon books. Jason, believe it or not, made $650 in a bad week as an introverted, shy, detail guy with little social ambition. Of course, the job did not last long, but imagine if Jason had been a Merchant type!

How do you guard against question chains? Pay attention to the questions. As soon as you have to give answers that the other side would already have known, watch out! The manipulation is happening. Respond in ways that are unexpected, such as, "I don't really like to reach my goals every tIme, thanks." Bam! Destroyed!

HYPOTHETICAL QUESTIONS

Imagine you are taking a cruise in the Bermuda triangle. The fire alarm suddenly blares while you are asleep in your cabin. Then, an explosion! Darkness. You wake up on a beach, unharmed. You start looking around. There are no other people around, just lots of debris.

You observe that the island has a rich natural bounty. Bananas and coconut grow right along the beach. It turns out that you somehow escaped disaster and ended up in paradise. Like Robinson Crusoe. Now, let me ask you, which famous

Hollywood personality would you like to spend time with on this lonely island? Daniel Craig? Scarlett Johansson? Thanks for your answer. I will keep it in mind.

Well, as luck would have it, let's say I later run into you and your partner in town in front of the theater. You introduce your better half to me. I say hello and ask if he or she was aware that their partner wants to spend time on a lonely island with Daniel Craig or Scarlett Johansson? Boom! Instead of reading this book, you are now leafing through a tome titled, 'How Do I Find a Steady Partner'.

Never answer a hypothetical question. The shipwreck was not real, the island paradise was not real, and I did not offer the choice of who could join you on the island. I certainly did not want you to say, 'my partner.' This question technique is common in journalism and politics, but also in sales.

Examples, you might recognize from your professional life are:

"Leaving the price aside for now, how do you like the design?" No, the price and the design are linked.

"Imagine our factory would be up and running in three months. Would you buy from us in that case?" Well, the factory is not finished, so no, I would not entertain that question. The next thing that could happen is that the same salesperson appears in my boss's office three months later and claims that I agreed to buy the product. The fact that is it was connected to the factory being up and running is long forgotten.

EMBEDDED QUESTIONS

Is your current project going as badly as your last one? If you answer with 'yes', your last project went badly and your current one, as well. If you answer 'no' (which I expect), you probably meant to reject the insinuation that both projects went badly. But what you are actually saying is that your last project went badly, but that your current project is doing better. So, in tomorrow's *Negotiation Herald* will be the headline: *Joe's last project went to hell!*

Never answer a question where one answer covers two questions. Always give two answers: No, my last project went well, and the current project is also going well.

CHAPTER 18: I Can Work with 'NO'! How?

Open-ended and closed-ended questions are critical techniques in communication strategy to use in any negotiation. While open-ended questions are designed to lure information out of the other side, closed-ended questions elicit a confirmation or denial from the other side. Both types of questions are important in a negotiation.

OPEN-ENDED QUESTIONS

If you are in a situation of relative weakness, you have to find out what the other side is bringing to the table. Open-ended questions are an important tool to use for getting that information.

Imagine looking at a pizza. I am holding it in my hand. It has a crunchy sourdough crust, a thick tomato base under three types of cheese. It is topped with pepperoni, mushrooms, basil, olives, bell peppers, onion... Can you picture it? Do you like my pizza? No! Oh, you are a vegetarian. What kind of pizza do you like?

Find out what delicious pizza your counterpart can bring to the table!

Do you notice the difference? When I described the pizza to you, I painted an image of a delicious pizza for you. I asked you a closed-ended question, "do you like my pizza?" This type of question will get you to confirm or deny my assumption that the pizza I described is delicious. You can answer a closed-ended question with 'yes' or 'no.' Closed-ended questions always start with a verb, "Do you…?" "Have you…?" "Can you…?" Etcetera. In my example of asking a vegetarian, the answer was "no." Then, I asked an open-ended question, "What pizza do you like?" Who is now painting the image? You are. And I am sure that pizza will be to die for. Open-ended questions always start with a question word such as 'who', 'where', 'when', 'why', 'what', 'which', and 'how'.

Two question words are particularly important for negotiations: 'What' and 'how'. 'Who', 'where', 'when', and 'which' are question words that do not require the other side to think very hard. The answers are simple pieces of information that they may or may not share with you. 'What' and 'how' are different. Questions starting with these two words require your counterpart to engage with you. "How can I do that?" Now you have engaged the counterpart in helping you find a solution. This type of question addresses a part of the brain that searches for solutions, not just facts. "What do you want me to do?" As with the 'how' question, this question does not allow a simple factual answer. Your counterpart is now engaged in finding a solution, a path to solving your problem. These two question words are a key to good negotiating.

For the parents among us who have raised children, we know this to be a sometimes mind-numbing fact: Small children ask open-ended questions. A child would never ask her mother a question like this:

"Do Kellogg's' Corn Flakes cost the same at Walmart as at Trader Joe's?" No. A child would ask:

"When can we get Corn Flakes, Mom?"

"Why is the sky blue?"

"Where does Grampa live?"

"When are we going the get to Uncle Joey's house?"

Children don't know, so they ask open-ended questions to acquire information.

Some of us, mainly The Merchant types among us (the personalities who thrive in contact and interpersonal relationship) will maintain their childlike curiosity throughout life. They also often find their way into sales jobs because they love to communicate, are good in establishing networks, and at maintaining relationships. They also ask great questions. A salesperson always wants to find that sweet win-win spot for a deal.

We have a natural disadvantage in the purchasing world. I have found a painful shortage of Merchant types in the purchasing departments throughout my years of coaching and training—and yes, Purchasing Managers, if you are listening, you need good communicators on your teams. Many buyers come from a technical background, maybe engineering, finance, or production. We are Scientists, Farmers, and Hunters. And, guess what? We don't naturally ask open questions. I am certainly guilty of the same.

As adults we have acquired information that tends to push us toward posing closed-ended questions. Many of us also are personalities that don't naturally ask open-ended questions. Buyers and managers often have an additional disadvantage: They are working for large corporations and are constantly reinforced in what they think they know: the structure, the plan, and the goal. Why ask the other side open-ended questions?

As corporate animals we have to be able to open ourselves up to the possibility that the other side might have a different plan than we do. We might still reach our goal, but not if we do not find out what the other side brings to the table.

If you, like me, are not good at asking open-ended questions, you have to practice. First, convince yourself that this is actually more difficult than you think. Use your spouse or a friend to help with this exercise: Ask ten open-ended questions in a row. Pick any topic. Note how many you asked before you slipped into a closed-ended question. Also, note how much you had to concentrate in order to ask open-ended questions. If you can do all ten questions without a problem, you are doing great. In my experience, Scientists, Hunters, and Farmers score somewhere between three and six open-ended questions before reverting to closed-ended.

Now that you know that this is not as easy as you thought, prepare three open-ended questions for each time you are planning small talk in a meeting, negotiation, or general conversation. Register the amount of information you are receiving, especially the parts you did not expect. This kind of conscious internal follow-up will help with giving your brain positive feedback. You will use open-ended questions more often as a result.

Make sure you allow the other side time to bring information to you. One of the most common mistakes I hear in asking open-ended questions is that the person immediately follows the open with a closed-ended question. Remember the pizza story? Following an open- with a closed-ended question shows that you really do not want to give up your idea of what a delicious pizza should look like. Here is an example:

"How much time will it take you to get the delivery to us?"

Then, without waiting for an answer, the immediate closed-ended follow-up:

"Ten days?"

What if the other side was about to say nine days? Or had a plan to airfreight some of the parts overnight and the rest in a week? Let your open-ended question linger; wait for the information to come to you. Silence is your friend, as it requires the other side to respond. The French composer Claude Debussy once gave a great definition for music: "Music is the space between the notes." Give the other side the space to think and assemble information, or, even better, work on solving your problems. Then, use that information to ask the next question. Suddenly, you are steering the conversation, while the other side thinks it is doing all the talking.

Open-ended questions are one of the easiest tools to use in negotiations. The common rule in sales training is to listen eighty percent of the time, and speak twenty percent of the time. That ratio is the same for purchasing, especially if you are negotiating from a position of relative weakness. Think about your position in a negotiation against a monopolist. The other side does not have to make a deal with you. Who is the salesperson in this scenario? If it's you, then you have to act like one.

Closed-ended Questions

Is there a strategic place for closed-ended questions? Of course, there is. If you want your counterpart to admit to a quality problem, you can nail them to the wall with well-placed closed-ended questions. Most of us know and use this inquisitional line of questioning.

More suitable for our goal of using effective tools in a weak bargaining position are closed-ended questions that mirror what the other side says. Mirroring is a simple technique to make the other side feel that they are heard. For example, my counterpart says,

He: "I took three international trips last month."

You: "Last month?"

He: "Yeah, all in a month. It was quite exhausting, especially because of the different time zones."

You: "Different time zones?"

He: "Six! On one of the trips to Taiwan, the difference was 13 hours. I did not even know that that was possible."

Can you tell, how your counterpart now feels empowered that you listened to him? You can use this technique (sparingly)

to elicit more information and keep the counterpart engaged. As a general rule, try to repeat the last three to four words of your counterpart's statement.

Another psychological technique that makes the other side feel understood, and helps de-escalate conflict, is called labeling. You basically call out an emotion that you can sense in the other side.

He: "Your company pays no attention to us. Just last month I tried a dozen times to get your quality guy to come here!"

You: "I understand that you are angry. I am here to give you exactly what you need."

He: "You can send your quality guy to us?"

You: "No problem."

You can tell how the simple labeling of the emotion, anger, diffused the aggressive nature of the conversation. Labeling starts with words like "It seems that you are angry, disappointed, frustrated...", "I can sense your frustration, anger, disappointment...", or "I understand that you feel disgusted, abandoned, upset...".

While mirroring can become very obvious very quickly if you overuse it, labeling is generally a great technique in dicey situations where emotions stand in the way of finding a solution. You communicate cooperation, empathy, and understanding. You can also use this technique to blame an authority not in the room, and thereby deflect the emotion to this unseen entity.

You: "It seems that you are disappointed in us."

He: "You bet, why do I never get a response?"

You: "My boss has been going through a divorce. He has not been himself lately."

He: "I sure could tell."

There is also a deeper, more psychological dimension to closed-ended questions. In Sales, we are taught to pursue the 'Yes,' to be pushy and direct the conversation to get the ultimate agreement. So, we ask a ton of open-ended questions, elicit the necessary information to drive to the end, then put that proverbial bow on the bag with the essential closed-ended question: "So, do we have a deal?"

'Yes' does not necessarily always mean what we think. Have you ever tried to get someone off your back and the only way to do so is by saying 'yes'? Of course, that type of 'yes' is non-committal; in fact, you already decided you will never do what you just agreed to.

I once negotiated with a famous Mexican writer about the English rights to his books for my publishing company. We talked through a host of issues. He reminded me, for example, how much publishers in Mexico paid him for advances, to which I responded how much investment good translations require. We ended up agreeing on terms and concluded the meeting with a handshake. I sent a contract to him a few days later. He never signed it. After pushing for months, I confronted him. He explained that he never intended to abide by our agreement. Why did he say 'yes?' Because it got me off his back. A direct 'no' is considered rude and unfriendly, especially in Latin and Asian cultures, so his 'yes' was simply part of his negotiation. I did not understand that until much later.

Beware if someone across the table says 'yes, yes,' eyes shifting, and feet pointing to the door. You do not have an agreement; or if you do, it will not last. It will be sabotaged, hollowed out, and more trouble than it is worth. So, we want to elicit the committed 'yes'. How do get that? I know it sounds odd, but you need to start with 'no' to get the good 'yes'.

'No' is actually a good answer. Think of it this way: You are allowing your counterpart to tell you what they don't want. Now they are in control. The sense of control helps with commitment.

"Have you thought about maintaining the pump?"

"No."

"Do you want to replace the pump every five years?"

"Of course not. Can you provide preventive maintenance?"

"Sure."

"How much is it?"

Now an annual maintenance contract is their idea. Your counterpart went exactly where you wanted them to go, but they felt in control. That is an excellent use of closed-ended question techniques. Elicit a 'no' before you try to get to 'yes'. Now you have a commitment that you can count on.

CHAPTER 19: The Free Child and Other Playmates

There is a German saying that, loosely translated, means: As you shout into the woods, so it echoes back out. It means in communication that for every action there will be a reaction. We do not communicate in a vacuum.

The Canadian psychiatrist, Eric Berne, created a brilliant model in the 1950s that helps explain the impact of personality 'shares' in the context of communication. He called that model 'transactional analysis'. The basic question of communication is what happens when two people interact verbally. Let me illustrate the model with a simple scenario. And, please forgive me, psychologists among us, for simplifying this grand theory in the service of practical negotiation tools.

Question: "What time is it?"

Answer: "3:30 PM."

Let us assume that it was me who just asked the question, and you who answered it. This quick communication consisted of two transactions. I asked for the time, and you gave me the answer. Even better, the answer you gave me was exactly what I expected. Let's call that good communication. I took a risk when I asked you, though.

Instead of giving me the correct time, you could have said:

"Go buy yourself your own damn watch!"

Or you could have smiled at me and said, "What a great question! I posed that question to ten people yesterday, and they all gave me a different answer."

See, there could have been answers that I did not expect, and that I also did not want to hear.

Eric Berne developed the idea of each person acting and reacting from what he calls 'Ego States'. Using Berne's model, my question about the time and the three different answers came from different ego states.

There are three ego states in transactional analysis. The Child, the Adult, and the Parent. See the following graphic:

Ego States

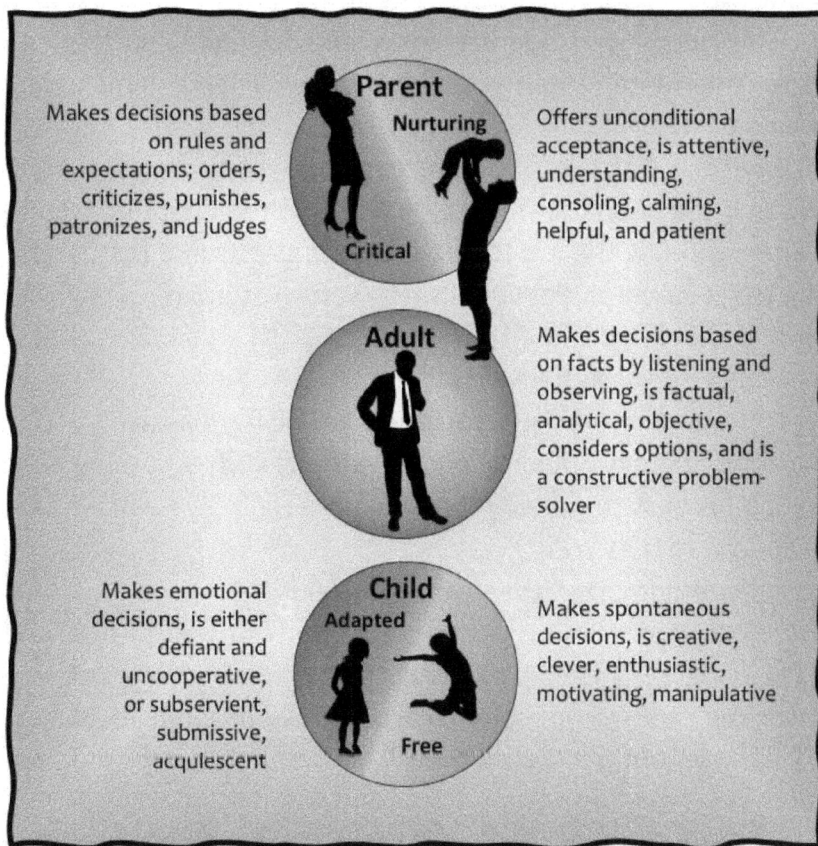

Makes decisions based on rules and expectations; orders, criticizes, punishes, patronizes, and judges

Parent
Nurturing
Critical

Offers unconditional acceptance, is attentive, understanding, consoling, calming, helpful, and patient

Adult

Makes decisions based on facts by listening and observing, is factual, analytical, objective, considers options, and is a constructive problem-solver

Makes emotional decisions, is either defiant and uncooperative, or subservient, submissive, acquiescent

Child
Adapted
Free

Makes spontaneous decisions, is creative, clever, enthusiastic, motivating, manipulative

Figure 8: Ego States

Let's start with the child ego state. It contains two categories, The Adapted Child and The Free Child.

The Adapted Child makes decisions from an emotional background. If an Adapted Child acts from a positive attitude, it will submit and give in. Operating from a negative attitude, the Adapted Child rebels, but in a passive way. It is defying, block-ing, and vindictive. Adapted Child communication is common in work situations such as customer service, lower ranks of the military, and sales. If you remember our Personality Preference model, you might have guessed right that all personalities, save for The Hunter can operate easily and commonly in this ego state. The Hunter goes there only if his boss makes him, and he has no power.

Let me illustrate the difference between the uncooperative and the submissive sides of the Adapted Child. Imagine a waiter who has the job to serve dinner guests in a restaurant. The job requires professionalism toward customers, even in situations that are beyond their control.

"The soup has a hair in it!"

"I am sorry! I will get you another one right away."

The apology could be truly meant as such and the waiter will do his best to remedy the situation. He brings a new plate of soup.

"Now it is cold," the guest complains.

"I am sorry, Sir. I will take it back and bring you a new one right away." He goes into the kitchen. If you, the guest, are lucky, the chef will not spit in the next bowl of soup. The waiter now comes out and "accidently" spills the entire contents on you.

"Gosh, so sorry," the waiter says. There is the defiance of an Adapted Child.

It is important in any communication to look at which ego state each ego state addresses. That does not mean that the answer is coming back from the addressed ego state, but that is the number I am dialing. The Adapted Child can only address another Adapted Child ("I am sorry!" / "I am sorry, too!"), or the Nurturing Parent ("I am sorry!" / "Don't worry.").

The Free Child reacts in from a completely different perspective than the Adapted Child. Rather than submitting to its environment, it breaks out of the pressure it faces through spontaneous creativity. The Free Child's enthusiasm and motivating manipulation sweep the other side up to participate rather than to object.

Let's revisit the question about what time it was and the answer, "What a great question! I posed that question to ten people yesterday, and they all gave me a different answer."

That answer came from the Free Child.

According to Berne, Free Children only communicate with other Free Children. ("Let's go swimming!"/ "Great idea, I'm coming!").

Free Child communication is common in sales, advertisement, the arts, and entertainment. In the Personality Preference model, The Merchant is most often in this ego state. I work hard in my consulting engagements on getting Hunters to adopt this mode of communication. By nature, Hunters are highly motivated, can think out of the box, and can motivate others, if they communicate from the Free Child ego state.

The Adult is the ego state that is unemotional. Decisions derive from facts. The Adult considers options, responds objectively, and refrains from emotional outbursts. This communication primarily exists in technical or scientific work environments such as: engineering, research, medicine, legal work, accounting, and quality control. You probably guessed already that this is the ego state in which The Scientist is most comfortable.

The Adult only addresses another Adult. Just as the Free Child only wants a response from the same ego state, the Adult does not want any responses other than objective, analytical, and unemotional ("What time is it?" / "3:30 PM").

The Critical Parent has two sides in their communication patterns similar to the Adapted Child. The Critical Parent enforces rules and commitments. The Critical Parent communication is critical or directing in that regard. As such, the

Critical Parent has the role of a protector, a positive control. The protective attitude can change rapidly when their counterparts do not meet expectations or fail to observe rules. Then, the Critical Parent communication switches to punishing, patronizing, and judging negatively. Now, the Critical Parent has switched to a negative controlling mode.

An example of these two distinct communication patterns is the following:

"Waiter, there is a hair in my soup! Tell your chef!"

"I am sorry, Sir! I will tell him right away."

"How is this possible! You have horrible service here!"

The first statement is critical, but in a positive way: "Tell the chef!"

The second part is patronizing with a personal attack on the waiter who probably did not put the hair into the soup. Therefore, the Critical Parent now engages in a negative communication.

Critical Parent communication exists in the work environment wherever power exists. Management, supervisory jobs, teachers, police, military ranks above private, all support this kind of communication. This ego state is the domain of The Hunter.

The Critical Parent only addresses one of two other ego states: The other Critical Parent, if talking about someone else ("The youth of today is really spoilt!" / "You're telling me! They're horrible!"), or the Adapted Child ("Why are you late?" / "I am sorry, it will never happen again.")

The Nurturing Parent is the supportive and cooperative side of the parent ego state. It represents the accepting, but non-subordinating communication of the parent. Nurturing parents want to engage in positive reinforcement while maintaining a clearly commanding role. A nurturing parent listens, shows understanding, is patient, calms the other side, and consoles.

Nurturing parent communication exists in the workplace where power exists, but is applied with empathy and positive reinforcement. Nursing, medicine, management, teaching roles all require the nurturing parent communication. In our Personality Preference model, The Farmer is most at home in this ego state. It allows them to explain their farm and nudge people to see the world their way. Since they are conflict-shy, they dominate through nurturing.

Just like the Critical Parent, Nurturing Parents address only other Nurturing Parents when talking about third parties ("I wish we could have helped Joe beat his alcoholism." / "Yeah, he is such a nice guy."), or the Adapted Child ("Let me help you with your homework." / "Thank you, Mom.").

COMMUNICATION PATTERNS

So far, this is quite theoretical. I am sorry for taking so much time to set up the practical tools (do you hear my Adapted Child?). I assure you that this tool is going to change the way you negotiate, especially the negotiators among us who have to do their work over the phone without the benefit of physical feedback. Communication has to be sharp and targeted. So, let's work this out! (Free Child communication).

Berne brilliantly defined three communication patterns to describe all communication.

Parallel Transaction 1

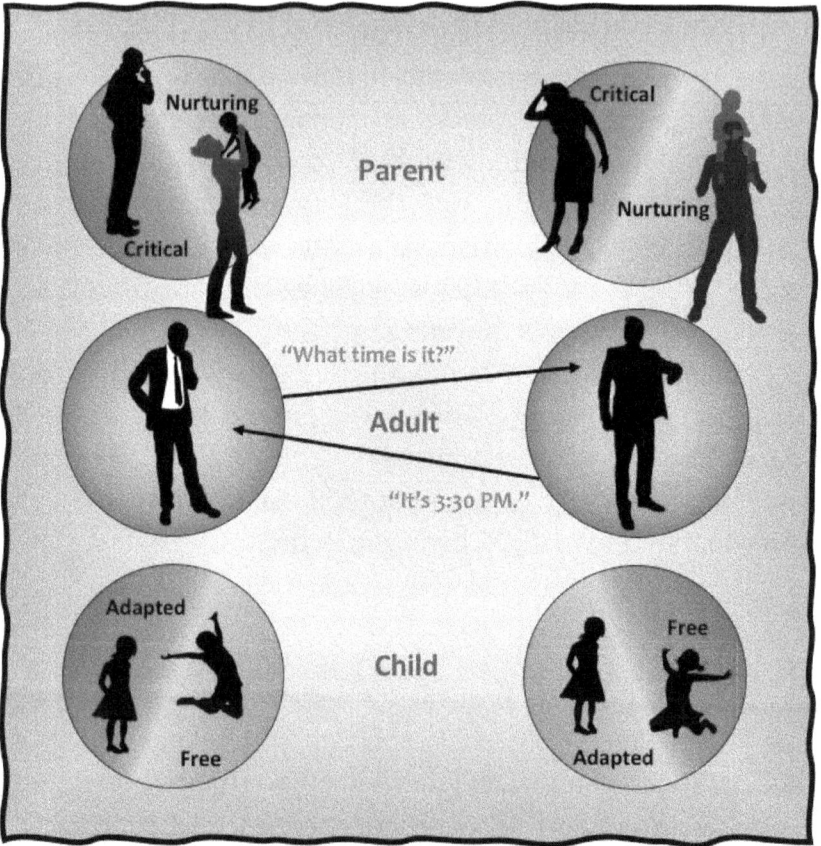

Figure 9: Parallel Transaction 1

A parallel transaction is good communication. The person addressing their counterpart addressed the correct ego state because the answer comes back as expected.

Person #1 asks from an Adult ego state: "What time is it?"

Person #2 answers from the Adult ego state and addresses Person #1's Adult ego state: "3:30 PM."

Another example, below, is from the Critical Parent ego state:

Parallel Transaction 2

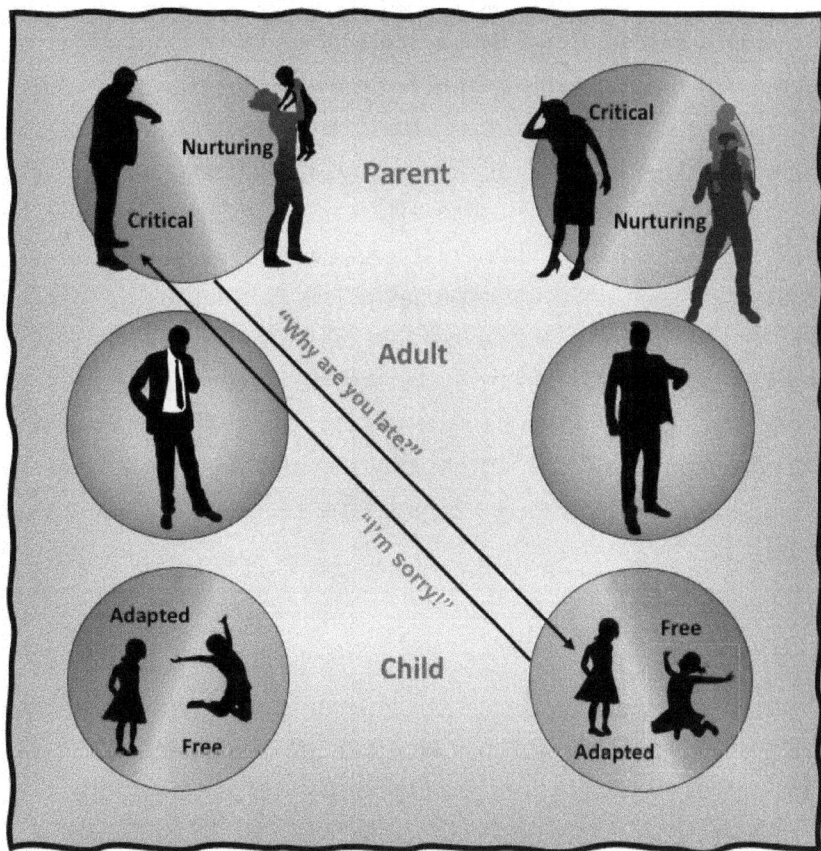

Figure 10: Parallel Transaction 2

Person #1 asks from the Critical Parent ego state: "Why are you late?"

He or she is addressing the Adapted ego state of person #2, expecting an apology.

Person #2 responds from the Adapted ego state, addressing the Critical Parent ego state of Person #1: "I am sorry."

The answer comes back as expected. Therefore, this is good communication.

You should always try to figure out which ego state the other side is addressing in order to create clear communication. If you address the other side, observe from which ego state the answer comes back. Try to find the parallel ego state. While this sounds really complicated and hard to implement, imagine the skilled salesperson who almost always finds the right ego state from which to communicate efficiently. Salespeople love to work from the Free Child ego state and always try to make you share their idealism and enthusiasm. It is contagious!

If you address a salesperson with good communication skills from a Critical Parent ego state, because you are in a bad mood, or simply like to use the power, they will always revert into the Adapted Child. You briefly win and feel good about it. Then, you are slowly suckered into the Free Child or Adult ego state.

CROSSED TRANSACTIONS

Crossed transactions describe communication where the ego state addressed is not from whence the answer comes back. This pattern typically describes friction in communications.

Crossed Transaction

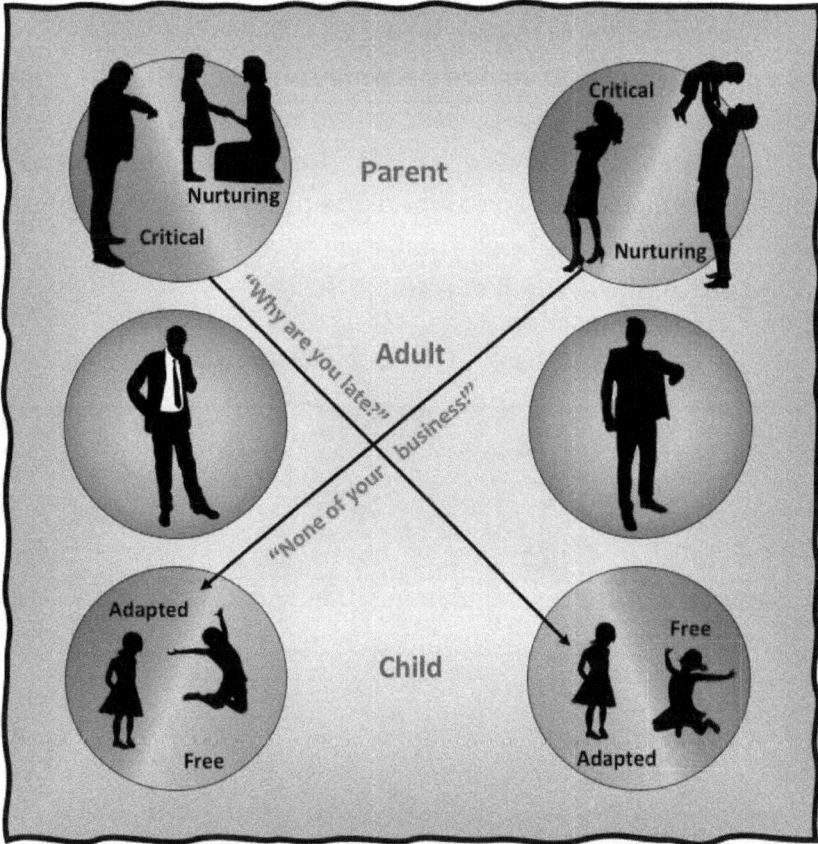

Figure 11: Crossed Transaction

Person #1 asks from a Critical Parent ego state: "Why are you late?"

Person #2, rather than answering from the addressed Adapted Child ego state, responds from its Critical Parent ego state addressing Person #1's Adapted Child ego state: "None of your business."

You can imagine how this conversation continues:

Person #1: "But I am your boss!"

Person #2: "You can't tell me anything!"

Person #1: "I will give you a written warning!"

Person #2: "You wouldn't dare!"

This can escalate as the communication continues Critical to Adapted, Critical to Adapted, Critical to Adapted...

How do you prevent a fight? One of the two people communicating has to go to where the other side expects them to be. Even if it is very brief. Then, the conversation has to move to the unemotional Adult ego state.

Resolving a Crossed Transaction

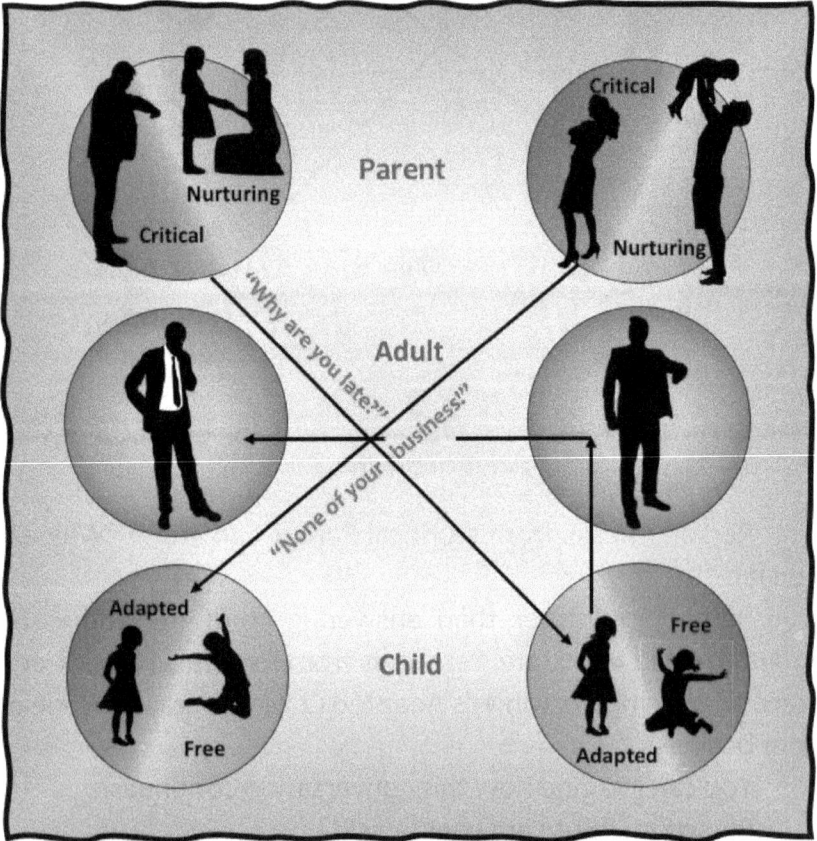

Figure 12: Resolving a Crossed Transaction

To go back to our example:

Person #2: "You wouldn't dare!"

Now Person #1 briefly goes into the Adapted Child ego state, and then moves the conversation to an Adult ego state.

Person #1: "Look, I am sorry to have upset you so much (Adapted Child). What happened this morning (Adult)?"

Person #2: "My wife had an accident and I had to take her to the emergency room (Adult)."

Person #1: "How bad are her injuries? Which hospital is she in (Adult)?"

The situation is now de-escalating. The fight turned into parallel transactions. This is a critical tool in any negotiation where emotions run high. A good negotiator is always able to recognize being stuck in an ego state and break out of it using sentences such as these:

"I see your point, but..."

"I am sorry this happened to you. Let's look at..."

"You are right. Here is what..."

"You are in a tough spot. Why don't we..."

"I understand why you are upset. Let's go back to..."

Using the approach of briefly adopting the Adapted Child mode to then move the conversation to the Adult ego state will make the other side feel that they have succeeded. It is also possible to go straight to the Adult ego state, but it sounds abrupt, and because it is usually not smooth, it may not work in getting the other side into the same ego state.

HIDDEN TRANSACTIONS

Hidden transactions describe conversations in which people say something different than what they mean. A hidden message takes cover behind the objective words. This pattern describes communication that encompasses sarcasm, cynicism, and humor. Here's an example:

My wife comes into the kitchen. She opens the cabinet door underneath the sink. She calls to me:

"The trashcan is full!"

I respond, "Yes."

Fifteen minutes later, my wife comes back into the kitchen. She opens the cabinet door again. Now she is mad.

"Damnit, you still haven't emptied the trash!"

You laugh. See, this is how humor works on its most basic level. You knew that there was a hidden message.

When she said, "The trashcan is full," I understood her addressing me from the Adult ego state. What she really meant came from the Critical Parent: "Do your damn chores!"

Hidden Transaction

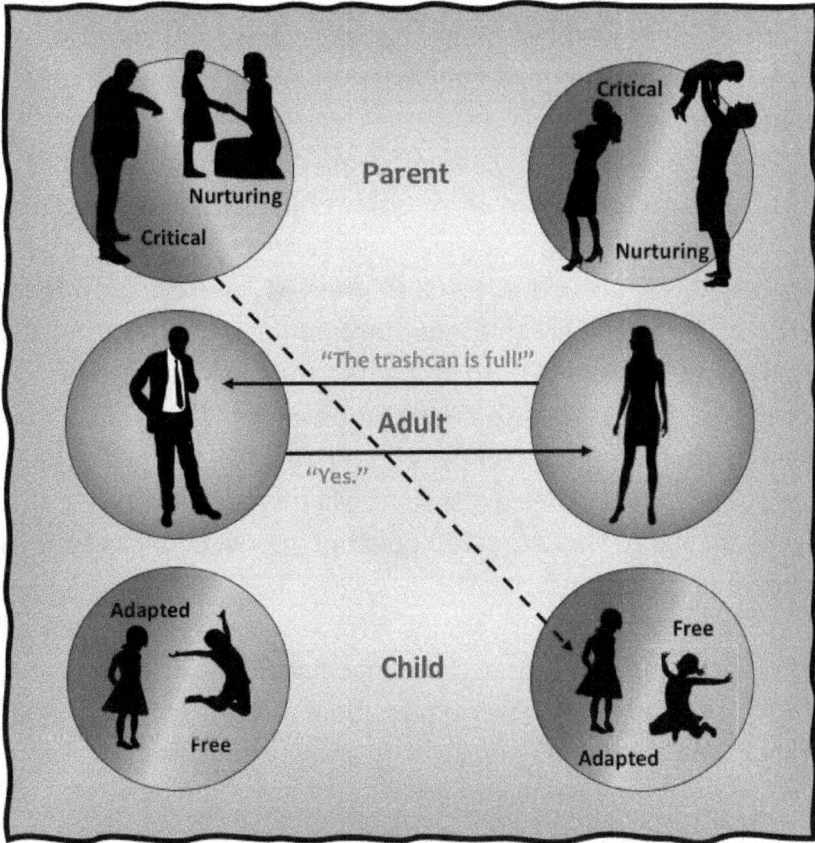

Figure 13: Hidden Transaction

How do I recognize hidden transactions? The response comes from an unexpected ego state. This communication is also not productive. It is disrupted as a result of the hidden messaging. This pattern has taken on special importance for me in my work as a coach in many international settings. Hidden transactions also lead to misunderstandings. This is especially true of situations in which the negotiators have different native languages; both sides have to be keenly aware when responses come from unexpected places. As a sidebar, never try to translate a joke from another language. Not all cultures interpret hidden transactions the same way. You run the risk that your translated joke generates an awkward silence rather than a good laugh.

Let me give you an example from a negotiation in which I participated. I presented an ambitious business plan to a group of executives. The participants all came from the southern United States. I was the only foreigner. My presentation team included an engineer, an accountant, and a manager from the Quality Department. After I presented the business plan, it was time for the executives to ask questions.

The owner of the company spoke first.

"How much initial investment will this take?"

I answered this expected question easily. Other questions followed.

Then, the owner again: "Have you thought about staggering the acquisition of the machines?"

I offered a quick explanation why, from a profit standpoint, this would not save any money but delay the return on investment by twelve months.

He nodded: "Good point. Nice work, Harry."

I was elated. The meeting had gone well. Everyone smiled and nodded. The owner promised a quick decision. I walked next to the engineer who was a good friend of mine as we filed out of the conference room.

"Hey Bob, what did you think? It went great, don't you think?"

Bob looked at me in disbelief.

"Great? I don't think so. They will never do it."

I was shocked.

Well, it turned out they never approved the project. It required more investment capital than what the company could access. The owner had clearly communicated as much to everyone in the room. I was the only one who did not hear it. Why? Because in my native culture we do not learn to read between the lines, and I missed that hidden transaction. Germans are direct and, therefore, often perceived as rude. A southerner would never say, "Harry, this is a horrible idea, go away," whereas a German might.

Let me sum up the tools you can derive from this model:

Parallel transactions are your friend!

- Make sure you are sensitive to addressing the expected ego state and subtly moving the conversation to the ego state through which you have the best chance of convincing the other side.

Free Children make the best playmates

- if you are in a position of weakness. Pull the other side away from the Critical Parent or the boring, unenthusiastic Adult mode. Show excitement, creativity and motivation, and watch the other side join you. The only personality where you will have trouble doing this is The Scientist. If they don't like your exuberance, stay in the Adult ego state for them. For the Hunters among us, here is your ticket to get salespeople to eat whatever you're selling right out of your hands. You are powerful, you are motivated, you have exciting goals! So, get away from that Critical Parent role and the pressure-addicted dictatorial position, and move to the Free Child. Your employees and negotiation partners will love you for it!

The Adapted Child helps deescalate!

- When crossed transactions zap through the room, give in for a quick second. Learn the magic words that calm the other side down. Then, take the conversation to where you want it to go. Especially, the Hunters among us have to learn that you lose nothing by showing a glimmer of understanding or regret. Only winning the war counts, remember? Not whether or not you won a bunch of battles.

Beware of hidden transactions!

- Something else is going on, and you have to figure out what that is. Ask yourself, "Why am I being misunderstood?", "Why is the other side getting mad when I am trying to be nice?", "Why does the other side become defensive when I am not attacking?" Make sure you sharpen your sensitivity to answers coming from unexpected places. It might just be a simple misunderstanding. Then, ask a question that clarifies the confusion. Provide feedback about what you are perceiving. Deescalate the situation. You all might have a big laugh after you resolve the disconnect.

CHAPTER 20: The Tone Makes the Music – The Four 'I's

"The tone makes the music," my mother used to say, wagging her finger at me. What had I done? Probably what most teenagers do to challenge their parents: I was fresh, demanding, cutting, and snide. Parents of teenagers know that tone all too well.

I have been fascinated with tone of voice because there is so little written about it outside of its use in training animals. There are psychologists like Albert Mehrabian, of course, who coined the 7-38-55 rule (seven percent verbal communication, 38% tone of voice, and 55% body language). It is not a general rule of communication as it is often portrayed, but rather a rule of the influence of communication on creating an impression. Nonetheless, I subscribe to the idea that non-verbal communication takes up most of the conversational space, not the spoken word.

But, wait! What is tone if not voice? Let's define 'non-verbal' as not using words or speech. I think of music when I think of tone. We hear a song. That song has lyrics (verbal communication) and it has music (tone). One relies on the other to convey meaning. Both can be created, modified, and interpreted together and separately.

Why is this important? Most day-to-day negotiations in business happen over the phone, some even in writing via e-mail. The pandemic of 2020 will probably further detrimentally impact the frequency of face-to-face negotiations. So, while we discuss the depth of tone in a negotiation, please know I would always prefer to sit down with someone in person for an important negotiation. I would not want to miss the many cues and feedback a personal encounter offers.

Not having a face-to-face interaction creates a distinct disadvantage for the negotiators in that they cannot see each other and may miss important physical feedback. Yet, the reality is that most negotiations take place over the phone, although programs like Skype, Facebook, or Zoom facilitate a sort of hybrid to a real in-person meeting. A live conference via camera gives physical cues and feedback, but the delay of the signal does not make video conferencing a 100% substitute for the instant feedback of face-to-face discussions.

Most of what we discussed earlier in the book also applies to successfully negotiating over the phone or via video feed. Good preparation, understanding my goals and those of the other side, as well as using the correct strategy and tactics, all apply. Good verbal skills, question techniques, and staying fully connected also transfer well to distance negotiation. As a matter of fact, in indirect encounters success depends that much more on these tools being extra sharp, even more accurate, and precise.

The saving grace in indirect encounters is that there also is a dimension of non-verbal communication that has a huge impact on conducting a successful negotiation. According to

Albert Mehrabian, thirty-eight percent of communication is lumped together under the term 'Tone of Voice'. Tone is not what is being said, but how it is being said. I like to use the four 'I's to define tone: Inflection, Intonation, Intensity, and Instrument.

Inflection is the cadence and rhythm of speech, the emphasis placed on one word or syllable and not on another. Emphasis changes meaning, as in, "**I** have no energy." Or "I have **NO** energy." Or "I have no **ENERGY**." The same sentence can convey completely different meanings.

The question that begs an answer regarding negotiation is whether or not one can use inflection, and how to interpret it. Using inflection is the key to supporting the verbal argument (the lyrics). The rhythm of speech, the spaces between the notes (verbal), the pitch of the voice, and the key in which the music is played, are all choices we can make. I can lower my voice to sound calmer, or more competent. I can increase the pitch to sound more excited and energetic. Chris Voss, the former FBI hostage negotiator, defines his negotiation voice as the "late night FM DJ voice." A calming, soothing, non-aggressive voice that deescalates the situation, especially in a hostage crisis where lives are on the line.

Here are some useful methods for modifying and interpreting inflection:

How do you know someone is nervous? We already talked about the signals of stress, such as red cheeks and sweaty palms. I can also tell that someone is nervous by the inflection of their voice. Stress usually increases the speed of what is being said and jumbles the rhythm of the speech. If I am nervous going into a situation, then I purposely observe and modify my inflection. I slow down my speech and purposely build in gaps for reflection and allow the other side to react to what I said. This is a perfect spot for asking open-ended questions. If I want to use a calm and confident inflection, I choose, in musical terms, a six-beat, slow blues rhythm, extend my notes, reduce the number of notes, and purposely add spaces. Can you hear it?

Think of a negotiation that requires you to stoke up the other side in joining you in excitement to reach the goal. Your inflection should emphasize the verbal cues. Your rhythm should be faster. Gaps in the inflection are also helpful in this situation because you want the other side to go with you and feel your enthusiasm. Give them the chance to join you! A combination of open- and closed-ended questions confirming your energy make perfect sense here. "Would that not be fun?", "How do you feel about that change?", and "Exciting, isn't it?" are all good examples. Think of a Reggae song with syncopation, some fun solos, and a playful back-and-forth between the musicians.

Aggression and pressure also show in the inflection. If I am the aggressor, I can orchestrate my inflection in several ways. I can choose to speed up the rhythm of my speech and eliminate the spaces. Closed-ended questions will confirm my target, and whether or not the other side can accept it. I can also slow down in a threatening way, ask closed-ended questions, and use the gaps to build up the pressure on the other side. It depends on your authority and power levels. If you have a lot of both, the second choice might be more effective. If you are bullying, a faster pace might convince the other side. Think of a rock song, fast four-beat rhythm, screaming lead guitar, and intense voice.

Intonation modulates the sentence up, down, or up and down to infuse meaning into the words I am uttering. "How was the meal?"

"The fish (upward intonation) was good (downward intonation)." Meaning? Everything but the fish was bad. "The fish was good (upward intonation)." Meaning: I really liked the meal.

This dimension of tone is something hard to modulate but important to interpret. Intonation happens as part of normal speech. Falling intonation typically characterizes statements, commands, open-ended questions, and exclamations. Rising intonation happens naturally in closed-ended questions. It becomes more interesting when there is a rise-fall or fall-rise intonation.

A rise-fall intonation characterizes choices ("Are you upset or happy?"), unfinished thoughts ("How do you like your new boss?", "Well, he has a lot of experience…" Meaning: But I don't like him), and conditional sentences ("If he asks me, I probably should go.").

A downward, then upward intonation is always suspicious because it occurs when there is hesitation, reluctance, doubt, or uncertainty. Here are some examples:

"So, are you willing to confirm the delivery date?"

"Well, I suppose so…"

The downward inflection is on "I sup…" The upward inflection is on "…pose so…"

Can you hear it?

"Did you notify your boss of the delay?"

"I don't quite remember…"

The downward intonation is on "quite re…" The upward intonation is on "…member…"

Both examples express hesitation, reluctance, and passive disagreement. Be aware when that happens. Agreement, in this case, could be a tactic to get you off their back, rather than to cooperate.

Intensity describes the energy you place into your words to infuse meaning. High energy signals certain reactive emotions, like anger, surprise, fear, happiness, and disgust. Holding back energy could signal reflective emotions such as sadness, disappointment, contempt, and shame. Energy also signals motivation. An energetic tone projects excitement, commitment, power, as well as pressure and authority. A calmer, low-energy tone deescalates, soothes, reduces emotion, and exchanges it for facts and logic. Of course, the low-energy tone can also signal lack of commitment, boredom, and disinterest that comes across as arrogance.

New research is trying to come to grips with 'vocal fry', a vocal change among younger Americans that is becoming more and more prevalent. Creaky phonation, another definition of vocal fry, seems to come from popular music. The phenomenon exudes knowledge and a sense of not depending on the other side's opinion. It can communicate arrogance and lack of interest.

None of these signals happen in a vacuum when you meet face-to-face. But you can easily appreciate the potential for misunderstanding and misinterpretation of tonal signals without the complementing body language. In music, intensity is one of the most important tools of the composer. Increasing intensity of both, volume and voices, projects tension, buildup to a solution, and emphasis. Decreased volume projects finesse, sharpens the attention to detail, and invites reflection.

These traits fit perfectly into our environment of negotiation and the purpose of intensity. We have a lot of choices here to modulate the tone, how we emphasize and build up energy, then tickle the interest of the other side with low volume, and quiet speech. Take the time and listen to The Four Seasons, a beautiful classical piece by Antonio Vivaldi. Think of your speech when you soak in the finesse of the orchestration, and the use of intensity as a means by the composer to mesmerize you.

Instrument characterizes the vocal traits. For the most part, the instrument is physiological, but not entirely. A team of researchers studied whether or not vocal characteristics of political candidates influence voters' attitudes towards them. They concluded that "males with lower-pitched voices tend to be perceived as more attractive, physically stronger, and more 'dominant'..."[5] We know from an evolutionary standpoint that the lower pitched male voice communicates good genetics and sexual ability. It attracts women and creates a sense of competition, but also respect, in men. The researchers also found that for "females, the standard is dichotomous: Women with higher-pitched voices tend to be considered more attractive, whereas those with lower-pitched voices are perceived as more dominant."[6]

Think of the voices that fit these descriptors: Brittle (emotional, about to cry), Gruff (tough, unfriendly, strong), Wobbly (afraid, nervous), Flat (unemotional, detached, factual),

---

[5] "Candidates' Vocal Characteristics Influence Voters' Attitudes Towards Them," by Casey A. Klofstad, Stephen Nowicki, Rindy C. Anderson, *American Scientist*, September-October 2016, Volume 104, number 5, page 282.

[6] Ibid.

Husky (sexy, appealing), and Honeyed (false, deceptive, artificial).

Pitch is a voice trait I can modify to a certain degree. We are given a certain pitch naturally, but to use the early example of music, I can change the pitch of a guitar, piano, or stand-up bass within a certain range. I just can't make a stand-up bass into a guitar. Let's go back to earlier examples of inflection and add pitch to the mix. If I am nervous, I will naturally increase my pitch. If I want to sound calm and relaxed, I can purposely lower the pitch of my voice. When I am excited, my natural voice pitch will go up. To reflect excitement and enthusiasm, I can purposely increase my pitch to emphasize the energy of my argument. Using pressure allows me to decide what pitch will support my strategy. A lower pitch communicates power, confidence, restraint, and a higher pitch anger, emotion, and aggressiveness.

Every person also has vocal traits that they cannot modulate. In radio, film, music, or theater, directors select certain vocal traits to fit a specific purpose. While a select few can modulate vocal traits, most people are either a tenor, baritone, or soprano. You might know the deep, soothing voice of the Allstate Insurance guy from TV commercials, the sinister voice of Jack Nicholson in *The Shining*, the energy-bursting babble of Robin Williams in *Tootsie*, or the inquisitive, understated whispering of Julia McKenzie in *Miss Marple*. I interviewed several speakers for the audio version of this book (because my voice is too nasally and I have a fairly heavy German accent). I chose a distinctive voice, one that is energetic and modulated with a low pitch to connote competence. If you are listening to this book right now, what do you think? Did I achieve my strategic purpose?

Conveying the desired signal through tone is the issue when we try to crystallize the ingredients of tone into tools for our conversational skills. Tone reflects our mental state, just like body language, and comes from a subconscious part of the brain. If I am interested in the other person and I want to dispel doubt, anger, or fear, then I will modulate my tone to reflect that interest. I will use a soothing, deeper pitch for my voice, reduce my energy to speak calmly and with less volume, and add inflection that allows the other side space for reflection and response without time pressure.

I want the other side to stay connected when I have less bargaining power. In a partnership approach, I need to establish trust and openness to create willingness to cooperate. My tone has to be deliberately energetic to show enthusiasm and high motivation, not power and authority. I have to intonate downwards to empower my open questions. "How does that sound to you?" should have a downward intonation on the 'you' to avoid putting pressure on the person across the table. Expressions of empathy, such as, "How nice of you!" have a downward intonation on 'of you'. That creates the empathy.

The crucial question in every negotiation is whether my offer is good or bad, whether the other side has a willingness to accept or is rejecting. We will discuss all the critical cues to look for when you make an offer in the chapter on body language. Now, imagine how during a phone negotiation, tone of voice is the only cue you have to interpret, other than the verbal 'yes' or 'no' answer.

When you plan a negotiation, especially one that is not face-to-face, think of these multiple dimensions of tone, and evaluate which tone will advance your strategy the best: Funny (playful inflection, higher pitch, lots of energy) versus serious (even inflection, lower pitch, lower energy); formal (even inflection, lower intonation, lower energy) versus casual (playful cadence, high intonation, high energy); respectful (even inflection, lower intonation, medium energy) versus irreverent (lively inflection, high or low intonation, high energy); and enthusiastic (playful inflection, high intonation, high energy) versus matter-of-fact (even inflection, low intonation, low energy).

Here is an example of a serious, formal, respectful, and matter-of-fact sentence:

"I am sorry that you did not receive my last message."

A funny, casual, irreverent, and enthusiastic sentence could sound like this:

"I told my boss that 43.2 percent of all statistics are lies. You know what he responded? 'Are you 100 percent sure that these numbers are right?'."

How about serious, respectful, and enthusiastic?

"I am here to find a solution, Sir. And I have found a way out of this that you won't believe!"

These dimensions also correlate directly to personality, strategy and tactics, as well as, transaction analysis.

- ➤ Funny, casual, irreverent, and enthusiastic is The Merchant using The Free Child to pursue partnership
- ➤ Serious and matter-of-fact is The Scientist using The Adult to pursue either pressure or partnership
- ➤ Formal and respectful is The Farmer using The Adult or Nurturing Parent to pursue partnership
- ➤ Serious, irreverent, and matter-of-fact is The Hunter using The Critical Parent to pursue pressure or partnership depending on bargaining power

These transactions take place spontaneously during regular communication, and without much planning or analysis. In a negotiation you would be hard pressed to express every utterance with a pre-planned transaction analysis in mind. But being able to pause strategically, to evaluate which ego state you and your counterpart are communicating through, and to steer your course with purpose, may be a key to success in that negotiation.

CHAPTER 21: I Saw You Say Something

I am not a psychologist and don't pretend that I am. I am a professional negotiator and I am sharing the knowledge I gained over the years to try to determine what the other side is thinking, feeling, and experiencing. In the previous four chapters I discussed the seven percent of communication that is verbal and the thirty-eight percent that is tone of voice. Now, I want to address the fifty-five percent associated with body language.

Is it possible to understand and interpret body language without thorough psychological training? Of course, It Is! Over half of our communication happens in this realm and we would be severely handicapped if we could not understand it. This understanding, for the most part, is subconscious and this is where I want to intervene. Let's take our subconscious understanding of what people across the table are saying to us without words, and move it to the conscious part of our brain. Once we consciously understand what we are seeing, then we also can interpret the signals, draw conclusions, and adjust our reaction.

What I am not trying to do in this context is to make you hide your body language. When I train negotiators, I often use a camera to film mock negotiations. After I point out certain gestures and facial expressions, participants often use that feedback to attempt to hide their body language. Let me suggest that neither you nor I are good enough to do this in a believable way. My argument to support this statement? Have you ever watched a world championship poker game on television? What do the players wear? Shades, hats, and hoodies. If the most sophisticated poker players in the world need to cover their eyes and parts of their faces not to convey body language, I submit to you that neither of us can successfully suppress body language.

Body language is the expression of what you are thinking and feeling. If you experience certain emotions, they will reveal themselves in your face, gestures, eye movement, and posture. You can consciously correct specific issues that project body language signals. For example, I had a knee injury many years ago. Now, I cannot fold my left knee over my right knee. A psychological interpretation of why I suddenly fold my right over my left knee, therefore, is fundamentally flawed. I can't do it the other way around.

Another example is posture. Some people have bad postures due to back injuries, hereditary spine issues, or simply being comfortable in a slumped seating position. Once, I had a participant in one of my seminars who had his arms crossed over his chest all morning. I interpreted that he was signaling lack of interest—or even resistance. I focus on such things because I want participants to be open and ready to accept the information I am giving. So, I concentrated on this one person in particular. Even when I addressed him directly and got him to laugh, he remained closed. During a break, I asked him if everything was okay. He told me that he enjoyed the seminar very much, but that he was in pain. He had injured his shoulder the day before and was holding up his elbow with the other hand. He was not closed off at all.

In order to correctly interpret body language and draw conclusions from observations, it is crucial to realize that body language is an in-motion communication system. I cannot interpret what someone is feeling or thinking by just looking at that person. I have to see a reaction to something I did or said. Then the body language I observe has meaning. It is a reaction to what I just said and did. Take the example of the arms crossed over the chest. Someone might be comfortable that way, or, like my seminar participant, in pain, or someone else might be cold... There are many reasons why someone crosses their arms over the chest. However, if I say something to that person and the person reacts with crossing their arms across the chest or taking three steps back, or showing an expression of anger on their face, then what I just said provoked that reaction. That is information I need to absorb, interpret, and react to.

Can I manipulate body language? To a degree. Take for example that I cross my legs only one way because of an old injury. Since I know that and I do not want the other side to interpret my crossing the one leg facing them to mean blocking or rejecting them, I consciously do not cross my legs. I also have a face that people interpret as carrying an angry expression when I am thinking. That is the impression people get when I am actually in a resting position. Since I have received that feedback many times, I purposely smile, so the other side does not misinterpret my expression. If you have a bad posture based on reasons that have nothing to do with your mood, then tell the other side, so they don't misunderstand. If you have a bad habit of invading other people's personal or even intimate space and it has nothing to do with aggression, then dial it back.

What is personal space? In general terms, intimate space measures zero to two feet from your body, private space two to four feet, and social space between four and twelve feet. As you notice, the spacing is quite varied. That has to do with culture and personality. Southern cultures are typically less sensitive to invading personal space than eastern and northern cultures. As a German, my private sphere starts closer to three or four feet, whereas an Italian or Brazilian would likely consider that distance to be in their social space.

You can only manipulate reactive body language if you modify your emotions and thoughts. This is the secret of actors who, in a very believable way, can slip into situations and act as if they were real. As a matter of fact, a good actor believes the person they are playing in a specific situation is real. That is why the body language harmonizes with the assumed role.

The same is the case for the handful of people who successfully beat lie detectors: Although they lie, they trick their brains into believing that they are telling the truth. Only then will all the unconsciously released stress signals we discussed earlier take over the body.

So, what we want to learn is how to observe body language, consciously interpret it, and react appropriately to it. What is the key to observing? You guessed it! The light upstairs has to be on. You have to be fully engaged in order to consciously observe, interpret, and react.

FIRST IMPRESSIONS

Is there such a thing as a first impression? How does it manifest itself? Can it be manipulated? When a person meets another person for the first time, our brains are wired to create an immediate picture of the other person. How does this happen?

Billions of nerve endings focus on the other side. Our senses: smell, sight, touch (in a handshake), hearing, and taste are activated. The signals our brain receives through the sensory system flow through many filters. *Have I seen a person with that shape of nose before? What was that experience like? Negative? Okay, I don't like the person I am just encountering.* The same happens with tone of voice, facial expression, scent, and touch. We compare and contrast with previous experiences, and any prejudice we carry with us.

Is creating a first impression fair? Absolutely not. Just like my exercise with the four personality types, we are wired to stereotype and put people into premade drawers in a mental file cabinet. The initial encounter creates sympathy, antipathy, respect, disdain, fear, or excitement. If we could not stereotype on the fly, most likely our brain would be overtaxed. It would interpret sensual signals repeatedly to create a fresh picture of a person every time we meet someone for the first time. It is up to you to question your judgments and work on reducing fear of others, deep-seated discriminating impulses based on race, religion, culture, or any other blas.

Since we know that this is how our brains are wired, let's discuss some of the components that create a first impression and see if we can manipulate them. Picture a graph using a file cabinet that catalogs the quality of impressions. On the x-axis we plot competence, on the y-axis, sympathy. Given a scenario in which I use pressure for a negotiation, I am only interested in the competence scale. Sympathy does not matter. As a matter of fact, usually the pressure I am using prevents sympathy.

File Cabinet Model

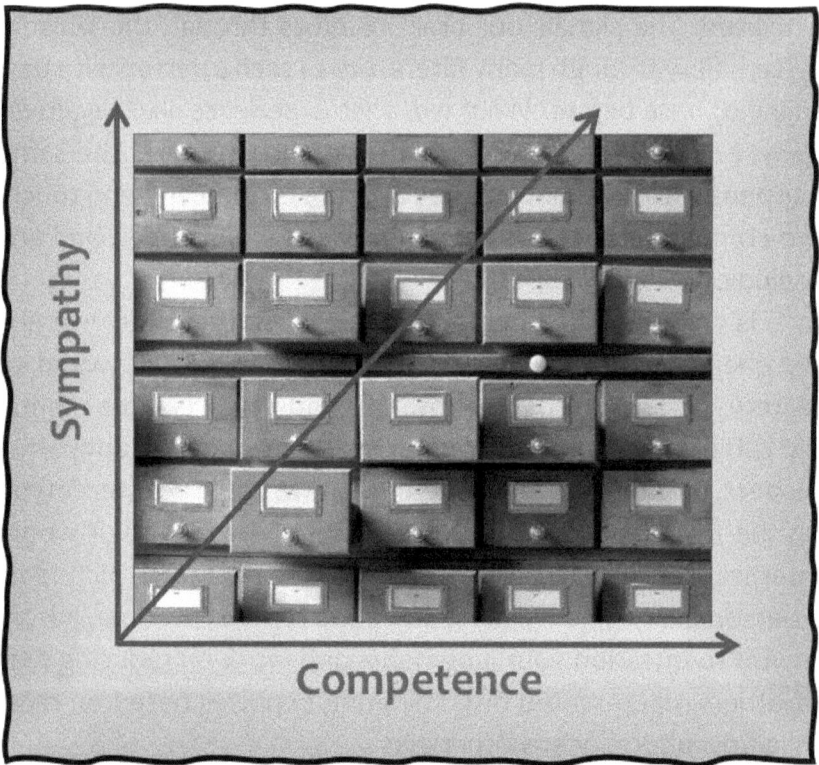

Figure 14: File Cabinet Model

However, if I am using partnership as a negotiation strategy, I want to land as high up as possible on the competence and sympathy scale. The higher up I can get as quickly as possible, the more likely it will be that the other side can agree with me. At this point, we need to exclude factors such as prejudice and negative previous experiences of the other side. We cannot help that very much, at least not in the short term. The short term is what we are interested in when negotiating. I only have a limited amount of time and I cannot waste it with trying to wrest myself up on that graph because my first impression was negative.

Items to consider when trying to influence the first impression are dress, smell, posture, facial expression, and handshake. How do I dress? We discussed dress briefly in the analysis of personality preference types. The Scientist is not interested very much in appearance. The Farmer will wear whatever he or she considers appropriate for the situation. If a corporate culture dictates a suit and tie for negotiations, then that will be what The Farmer will wear, in any negotiation. The Merchant will dress flexibly, often fashionably, but could also dress completely inappropriately to attract attention and spur conversation. The Hunter will dress fashionably and expensively. Appearance is important. A custom-tailored, expensive suit communicates success and wealth.

You can easily see that each personality type has ample opportunities to manipulate the first impression, but not always in their favor. Dressing sloppily, in a flashy manner, or inappropriately, will influence both competence and sympathy in people.

How I dress depends upon the situation I expect to encounter. If I am planning a negotiation with a supplier in a corporate setting, my appearance has to be professional, likely suit and tie or dress suit for women. If I meet a homebuilder about a window order and I am wearing suit and tie, both competence and sympathy will be low on their first impression chart. I look like I have never swung a hammer in my life! I may also look as if I have already made too much money, so why not try to beat me down even harder on price than planned. Dress is important. Pay attention to it.

Perfume and other scents also play a role in creating a first impression. A pungent smell, such as too much perfume or cheap cologne, can be offensive, communicates insecurity, lack of hygiene, and lack of taste. I have to admit that I have been in meetings where the scent from the other side distracted me a lot. The sympathy counter definitely went down rapidly.

A handshake establishes the first touch sensation between two people in virtually every professional encounter in western culture. A bow replaces the handshake in Asian cultures. The aftermath of the 2020 pandemic might change the cultural habit of shaking hands. Handshakes, however, do play a big role in our culture in creating a first impression. They are proof that we do not carry weapons. We have lots of sensors in our hands that check blood pressure, temperature, and muscle tension in the other side. We draw conclusions from those signals that inform our first impression.

Higher temperature, lots of blood flow, maybe even sweaty palms indicate stress. Stress could come from nervousness, so, as the counterpart, I may feel superior to the other side. It could also be the result of fear, especially the sweaty palms. I, as the counterpart, now wonder what induces the fear in the other side. Dishonesty? A lack of preparation? There goes the competence score!

Muscle tension also indicates level of energy, confidence, and power. A firm handshake will communicate confidence and power up to a certain degree. If overdone, the signal will turn to dominance which negatively affects the sympathy graph. I have heard from many female colleagues and clients how men try to show their dominance with an extremely tough handshake. If you are pursuing a partnership strategy for negotiation, you just blew it.

Example of a dominant handshake with a raised shoulder, and leaning into the counterpart

Posture also plays a role in the act of shaking hands. The right shoulder rising and the person moving into the other person's space from above, usually coinciding with the hand clasping the other hand from above, shows an attempt in dominance.

Pulling the other side to you in the process of shaking hands, not letting go for an embarrassing amount of time, or wrapping the other hand with you second hand are all attempts to dominate.

Example of a dominant handshake by pulling the counterpart in and grabbing their shoulder.

I mention this because, especially the Hunters among us, see nothing wrong with this. It is definitely a wrong move if you are pursuing a partnership strategy.

It is also dominant to grab the counterpart's hand and hold it with yours.

A submissive handshake is the opposite of what I just described. My palm is facing upward as I am shaking the other hand. Often, the submissive handshake coincides with a lack of muscle tension, or sweaty palms. This type of handshake might telegraph to the other side that I am weak, unenergetic, and somehow expect to lose. Weak handshakes negatively affect the competence and sympathy score. Try to shake hands in a neutral position, with the appropriate firmness, for the right length of time, and throw a smile into the mix for good measure.

A submissive handshake while looking away, with a hand facing upward.

A neutral handshake includes looking the counterpart in the eyes, and offering a straight hand with a smile, signaling friendly intentions.

That leads me to posture and facial expression. I can definitely manipulate the first impression with a smile on my face, a confident and upright stride, meeting the eyes of the other side to show trustworthiness and willingness to cooperate. We will now discuss the elements of body language that apply to all interactions, not just first impressions.

Remember, though, making a good first impression that supports the strategy you are pursuing in your negotiation is helpful. You don't have the time to climb up on the sympathy and competence graph. You need to start at the top!

POSTURE AND POSITION

The most basic observation about posture is whether it is open or closed. Again, remember that we can only interpret well whether someone is open or closed when they are reacting to something I have done or said. Closed posture, in general, means we are protecting sensitive body parts, the genitals, the abdomen and chest (our heart), and the throat. Since time immemorial, exposing those parts of our body could mean instant death. Covering those parts of our body are signs of a defensive, disinterested, or rejecting attitude.

What does a closed posture look like in real life? One leg crossed over the other protects the genital area. The leg that crosses usually becomes a block towards the other side. Often, the hands also fold together and rest over the genital area. Standing on one leg while using the other to protect the genital areas projects insecurity, a lack of balance, and vulnerability. However, if a person is taller than another, and that person stands on one leg, the imbalance can indicate self-assuredness and confidence. Crossed arms over the chest or abdomen also indicate a closed posture. People cover their vulnerable parts with things like handbags or briefcases, papers or files, jackets and coats. In the case of women, however, closed legs may have less to do with closed posture than with modesty and decency.

Example of a closed posture with feet crossed and body unbalanced.

A closed posture protecting private parts.

While a closed posture in which the other person is facing you usually shows a defensive or rejecting attitude, turning 'the cold shoulder' shows disinterest. A closed posture with the feet pointing away from you is a sign of disengagement or lack of interest. The feet pointing to the exit are a telltale sign of an activated flight motivator. The other side might be ready to leave.

A closed posture with the feet pointing to the exit.

An open posture exposes those vulnerable parts. Showing an open chest, abdomen, or an exposed genital area projects confidence, lack of apprehension or fear. If you observe the other side moving from a closed posture to an open posture as you communicate with them, whatever you said likely caused the other side to lose apprehension or opposition. They are now open to your argument. The open posture often also triggers the other side to assume a more comfortable position, like leaning back and relaxing visibly. This is an important signal to observe, especially in the small talk portion of the negotiation. Remember, how long should small talk last? Until the other side is at ease and relaxed. Then they are open to take in your information.

An open posture exposes the chest and sensitive parts.

Position sends a lot of signals to the other side. Facing away from a person, even if it is just the feet pointing away while the rest of the body is not, communicates a disconnect or disengagement with the other person or with what is being said. Watch for this signal when you mention another person and what is being said triggers a disengaged position. If you want to appear engaged and participating, you have to align your position to face your counterpart squarely.

An example of an open posture leaning forward to signal interest.

If the other side displays an extremely open posture, such as leaning way back, legs wide open, and a direct stare into your eyes, that is not an indication of ease and relaxation. That is a signal of aggression, as if to say, "give me your best shot, Pip Squeak!"

This posture says, "Give me your best shot!"

Some other important signals that posture sends are the inclination of the body, as well as the position of the head and shoulders. A hanging head and lowered, forward sloped shoulders indicate a lack of confidence. Lowering the head portrays lack of motivation or feeling beaten up by some higher power (like the boss). It could indicate shame, as the person with the hanging head feels uncomfortable with their arguments or actions. Shame usually coincides with looking to the ground or not being able to look the other person in the eyes.

A body that is hunched forward can project the same feeling of the environment weighing heavily on that person. A slight forward inclination of the body in a conversation projects interest, acceptance, and sympathy. A rapid forward inclination of the body, especially if that movement invades your personal space, is a sign of aggression. An inclination away from another person signals dislike, disapproval, or a defense against a perceived aggression.

Pride, confidence, and self-assuredness usually displays in an upright posture, shoulders back, head held high, both feet on the ground. If you want to influence the first impression the other side has of you, working on a confident posture certainly helps.

This confident posture shows a straight body, with hands visible, feet firmly planted on the ground, and head held high.

HEAD MOTION

We move our head to convey lots of messages. The most basic head movement is nodding or shaking, meaning 'yes' or 'no'. At least most of the time. Nodding your head often just means, "I hear you," and is not an agreement. Very pronounced head-shaking, in Asian cultures especially, leads to many misunderstandings in people who grew up in western cultures. Indian people usually show a side-to-side movement of the head to convey agreement. The same movement of the head in a western culture would indicate indecision, such as maybe, could be, let's see...

A head held high shows confidence, a hanging head lack of it. The head turning sideways, maybe angling for the exit may indicate that for the other side the conversation is over. A bouncing head can indicate contemplation. It usually coincides with the mouth angling down. We will discuss these facial expressions later in the chapter. A head angling sideways indicates interest and curiosity. A sudden upward movement of the head signals a positive surprise or sudden attention. A sudden backward movement might indicate disgust or a negative surprise. The head sinking into the neck with the shoulders going up means "I don't know." This posture usually coincides with the arms extending with the open palms facing upwards.

A head held high displays arrogance, looking down on the counterpart

The head slightly tilted shows interest.

The head sinking into the shoulders says, "I don't know."

I pay close attention during a negotiation to non-verbal interactions between two negotiators that sit across from me. Non-verbal hand-offs usually only work with head and eye movements. One negotiator will look at the teammate to search for permission. Now you know who the decision maker is if you didn't know by then. You can actually force that scenario if you ask one of your counterparts a direct question. If that person answers without looking to the other team member, you have the decision maker. If the person you addressed looks for permission or even hands the question off to the team member, then that is your decision maker.

Searching for agreement or permission in the teammate also indicates whether or not the team agrees. If not, you may be able to use the disagreement to your advantage. Agreement usually displays as a nod or a blink of the eyelids when the two teammates look at each other. Disagreement could be a quick display of anger, shaking of the head, or often times, the teammate will refuse to look over.

GESTURES

I'll keep this part brief for the purpose of providing a short, but helpful, collection of common body language. I am only interested in gestures that convey thinking, feeling, and state of mind, not emblematic, such as replacement of words, or sign language. We all know the signs for 'okay', 'thumbs up', 'thumbs down', the Vulcan greeting, and such. Gestures mostly underscore the spoken word, but at times they convey important differences between what is said and what is actually happening inside the head. Our radar should become especially active the moment we observe that the body language does not correlate with the verbal communication. Something is not truthful about what the other side says.

During a negotiation, I am looking specifically for gestures that show frustration, contemplation, agreement, aggression, rejection, nervousness, expectation, furtiveness, trust, and honesty. I always contrast the gestures I see with what is being said. If they do not coincide, I pay exceedingly close attention. I am also on the lookout for what I call 'transitional gestures'.

A decision usually comes after some contemplation, either positive or negative. Retreat or aggression usually follows frustration. These transitional gestures are especially critical in the moment I make an offer. In that split second of receiving the offer, the other side will betray their thoughts through body language, unless they are incredibly sophisticated. Only in that split second. Because right afterwards, the conscious brain takes charge and the body language may no longer be authentic.

Let me explain the two most important transitional gestures: Frustration and contemplation.

Frustration usually expresses itself in the gesture called the 'icebreaker'. Both hands touch each other as if in prayer and move up and down. If you notice the icebreaker pointing at you, and you did not intend to frustrate the other side, you need to intervene immediately.

This sign of frustration is called, 'The Icebreaker'.

Frustration will lead to either resignation, an attitude that might result in agreement, but could also produce an unwillingness to continue cooperation. Resignation and agreement usually display as exhaling, lowering the head, slumping the shoulders, then looking up. Agreement is near. If the looking down and slumping resolves into sitting back up and crossing arms across the chest (or any other move into a closed posture), cooperation has just ended.

Frustration can also lead to aggression. Your offer obviously hit a nerve. The icebreaker turns into a pistol, literally thumbs up with the index fingers over folded fingers pointing at the perceived target of assassination: You! Aggression also shows in leaning forward, raising the voice, clenching a fist, and using the index finger or an extension such as a pen to act as a sword slicing across your personal space. Your negotiation partner might have begun the process of losing his connectivity, lightbulb after lightbulb switching off. If that is not your intention and you want to maintain a partnership strategy, it is time to take a break... Now!

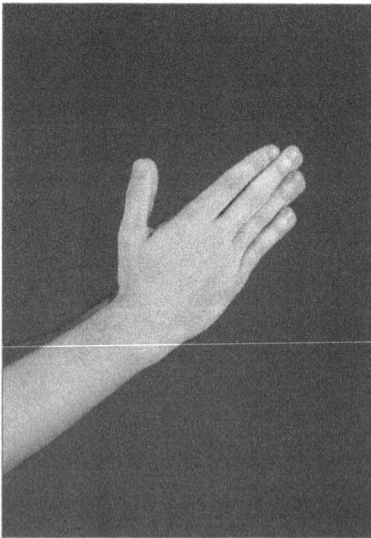

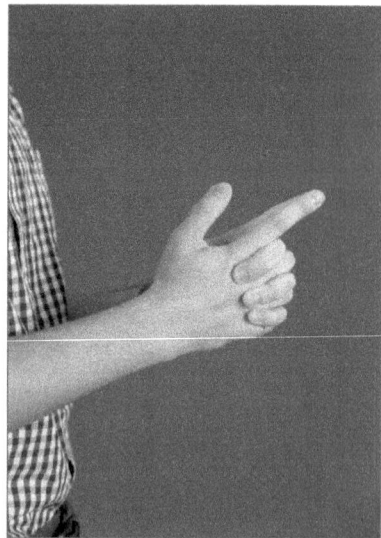

Here, 'The Icebreaker' turns into The Pistol'!

The other transitional gestures to watch out for are contemplation and evaluation. Typically, a person contemplating something will touch the chin of their face, sometimes resting the entire head in their hand supported by the elbow. German Chancellor Angela Merkel is famous for her contemplative gesture, which is the two thumbs touching and the two index fingers touching. The rest of the fingers are folded in. This makes a diamond shape form of the hands. Chewing in one side of the mouth also can indicate contemplation.

Touching the chin indicates contemplation.

'The Merkel' also indicates contemplation.

Was it a good offer or a bad offer? We don't know yet. That is why this gesture is so critical in negotiations. A decision usually follows contemplation. Will the next signal be positive or negative? We have to find out. A contemplative gesture often coincides with the head held at an angle, the eyes wandering to the recall side of the brain. We will discuss eye movement momentarily.

Contemplation transitions into either a positive or a negative reaction. Let's start with the positive responses: The person on the other side visibly relaxes, the posture opens, maybe a fleeting smile crossing the face indicates that the offer must have been good. You could also watch out for a nod or the literal thumbs up.

Negative reactions are the other result of contemplation and evaluation. Aggression is certainly a clear rejection of the offer: Leaning across the table, pointing an index finger, the pistol gesture, a direct stare, or an angry facial expression. Frustration also shows that the offer is not well received. Pushing the chair away from the table, covering sensitive parts, turning away, a swiping hand, as if to swipe the bad offer away, are all negative reactions.

Not too long ago, I filmed a mock negotiation during which the opposing side lifted up one hand, as if to say "Stop!" The movement was so quick that no one in the room watching the film noticed it. I replayed the scene in slow motion and there it was: A clear rejection that was immediate and lasted for less than a fraction of a second. If you are good at observing the other side, noticing these signals is priceless in a tough negotiation.

The hand says, "Stop!"

I try to determine trustworthiness of my counterpart in any negotiation. We will delve deeper into this topic in the next chapter when we discuss tools to detect lying. In general, it is critically important for me to see whether the other side is forthcoming or hiding something. If you have a habit of hiding your hands behind your back, in your pockets, or under the table, modify your body language. All of these signals indicate to the other side that you might be hiding something. It is an evolutionary trait that not seeing the other side's hands signal the threat of a weapon. An attack could be imminent. We are wired to think that way.

Hands in your pocket signal you may be
hiding something from your counterpart.

Hands under the desk signal holding something back from your counterpart

Hands behind the back may also indicate hiding something from your counterpart

Gestures showing honesty and trustworthiness are the hand on the heart as if to say, "I really feel that way." The open palms with outstretched arms literally show that the person is unarmed. You can see this gesture in church when the priest or minister engages in prayer. Open posture indicates trustworthiness, as well: "I have nothing to fear." Looking (not staring intensely) at the other side can indicate honesty. Dishonest behavior is stressful to most people, and they literally cannot look the other side in the eyes since the eyes are windows into our brain.

Open hands say, "No weapons."

A hand over the chest says, "Trust me!"

Hands on the desk say, "Nothing to hide."

Another gesture that draws my attention are the rubbing hands. What do they indicate? Expectation. Watch out, the other side has something planned and it is about to happen.

Hand-rubbing suggests expectation: "Something is about to happen!"

Nervousness is a signal for me to work on making the other side feel more at ease. I might increase my small talk and ask open-ended questions to learn why the other side is nervous. Nervous or uncomfortable counterparts will have a closed posture, covering vulnerable body parts, not looking one in the eyes, and feet pointing to the exit.

*A closed posture with the hands protecting
private parts is a display of nervousness.*

Gestures indicating nervousness, and even fear, include any kind of twitching (in the face or legs popping up and down), tapping, wringing hands, shifting in the seating position, scratching, biting fingernails, or playing with hair. If you are not sure why the other side is nervous or even afraid, it is your task to find out.

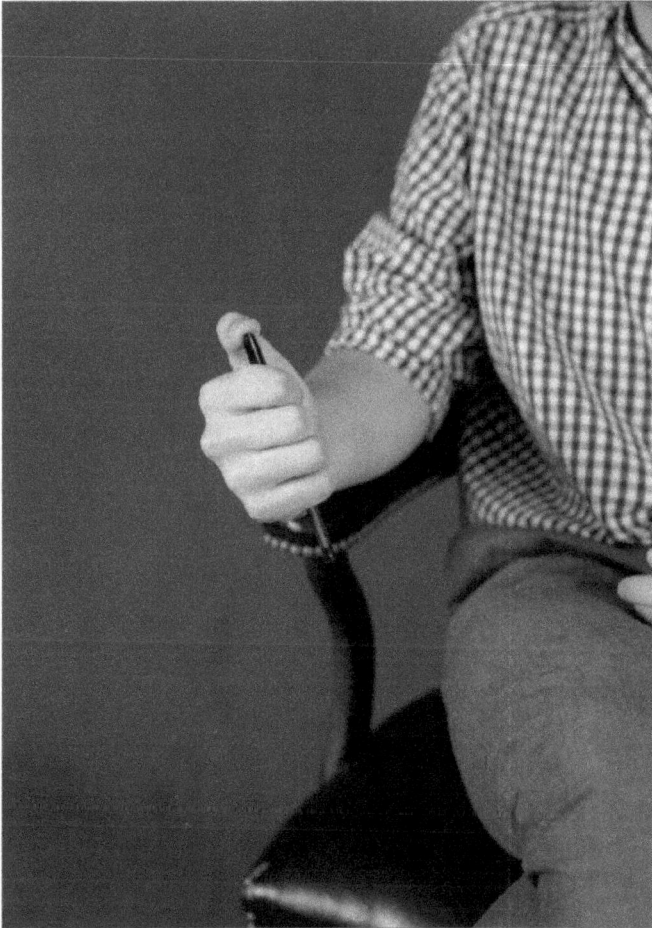

Other signs of nervousness include clicking a pen

A gesture indicating contemplation

Touching the face can also indicate a situation that I find particularly interesting in a negotiation. I already mentioned that touching one's chin indicates contemplation. The touch of the chin can move further into the face to cover the mouth. Oftentimes that means, "I would like to say something, but I won't."

The situation in which I find this gesture particularly interesting is when I am sitting across from two negotiators. One is speaking, the other covering his mouth. Boy, do I want to know what that person really wants to say, but is restraining themselves from revealing.

A hand covering the mouth says, "I could say something, but I won't."

A hand covering the face says, "I don't want to see it."

If the two across the table do not agree with each other, I have an opportunity to split the team and weaken their bargaining position. In a case like this, turn to the person trying not to speak and ask them directly. We already discussed other gestures that indicate disagreement in the head movement paragraph. You could also see one of the negotiators covering their eyes, as his teammate speaks ("I don't want to see this,") or the ears ("I don't want to hear this.").

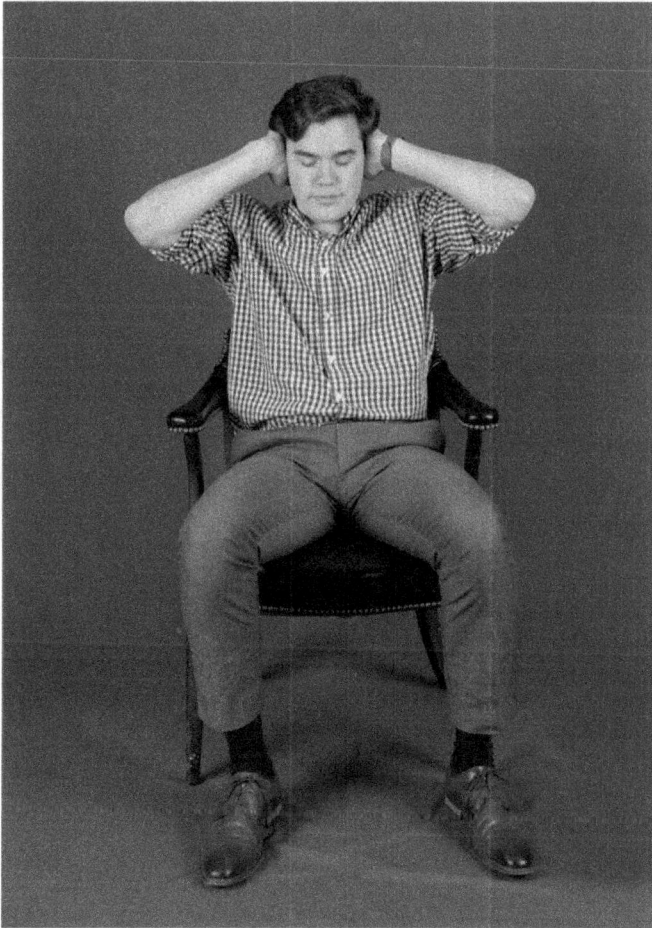

Hands over the ears say, "I don't want to hear it!"

EYE MOVEMENT

Students of literature know that eyes are the windows into one's soul. In negotiation, eyes betray which part of the brain a person accesses, and in a sense, what the person is thinking. Let's look into what each side of the brain controls in order to understand what the eyes have to do with our brain functions. The right side of our brain typically controls visual awareness, imagination, emotions, intuition, face recognition, music awareness, and left-hand control. The left side of our brain is in charge of number skills, analytical thought, logic, recall, written language, and right-hand control.

Eye movement is an involuntary and subconscious process, unless we have specific training in controlling it. The eyes will move towards the side of our brain that we are accessing at a certain time. We all have one side of the brain responsible for recall, another responsible for imagination. Typically, the right side of our brain controls imagination, while the left is in charge of recall. I cautiously say 'typically' because ninety percent of the population is left-brain dominant. Ten percent are either left-handed, which can mean that their brain side dominance is switched, or they are ambidextrous, which could mean that either the right or the left side of the brain are dominant.

During any negotiation I conduct, I ask control questions in the small talk portion of the meeting. These control questions are questions for which I am sure the other side knows the answers. For example, "Are you married?" "How old are your children?" "How long have you worked for the company?" All of these questions will prompt my counterpart to access the recall side of their brain. The eyes will wander most of the time to the top left, but in some cases, they will move to the top right. Either way, now I know where the recall side of the brain is. If I ask pertinent questions later in the negotiation and the eyes of my counterpart move to the imagination side... well, you might not be hearing the truth.

Let us imagine the face on the other side of the table and let's assume that we checked the recall side with a control question. We can now be reasonably sure that the right side of the brain is imagination, the left side is recall. This is what it means when the eyes wander:

Looking top left signals a visually remembered image. Looking left without going up or down means that the other side is remembering a sound.

Looking top left signals a visually remembered image;
top right, a visually constructed image.

Looking down to the left means that the other side is having an internal conversation, "Should I do this or not?" for example.

Looking right indicates constructing a sound; looking left, recalling a sound.

Looking to the top right means the other side is constructing, imagining an image. Looking straight to the right means that the other side is constructing a sound. Looking down to the right shows that the other side is constructing a feeling or an emotion.

Looking down and right indicates constructing a feeling; looking down left, an inner dialog.

Finally, a person looking straight at me usually means that they are looking for clues.

We will revisit eye movement again in the next chapter when we talk about how to detect lies.

Looking straight ahead means searching for clues.

FACIAL EXPRESSION

One of my personal heroes is Paul Ekman, a retired professor of psychology from San Francisco, California. He runs the Paul Eckman Group, a consulting and research company. The TV series, *Lie To Me,* is based on his work and business. Ekman invented the FACS system, the Facial Action Coding System, in the late 1970s. The system allows for a clear and unmistakable definition of facial expressions and their underlying emotions. The CIA, Department of Defense, as well as Disney and Pixar have used Ekman's work. However, Ekman's system is not without critics in the psychology and behavioral sciences arenas. I find FACS helpful for figuring out the most crucial question in a negotiation: Is my offer good or not?

Ekman identified seven basic emotions that directly correlate to the movement of specific facial muscles. We have forty-three facial muscles that the seventh cranial nerve controls. The FACS catalogues which combination of specific muscle movements relates to specific emotions we are expressing. The primary emotions include happiness, sadness, anger, fear, surprise, disgust, and contempt. Secondary emotions include shame, excitement, jealousy, guilt, pride, amusement, contentment, embarrassment, relief, and satisfaction. Here, we will concentrate on the seven primary emotions plus shame, which I found particularly important to recognize, for the purpose of identifying readily usable tools. The other secondary emotions are also recognizable with practice. So, use this tool and add the telltale signs of other emotions to your repertoire.

We all have the ability to read and interpret facial expressions, since they represent a large portion of our non-verbal communication. Let me describe the visual facial movement of each basic emotion. If you have children, observe their facial expressions for practice, since they are usually more expressive than grown-ups. It might also work to practice these seven expressions in front of a mirror. The more familiar you are with them, the easier it will be for you to identify them.

Happiness

Happiness expresses throughout the entire face, including the area around the mouth, the cheeks, and the eyes. The mouth angles upward, the cheeks push up, and wrinkles appear around the eyes, the so-called 'crow's feet'. The mouth can either be closed or open to display teeth.

True happiness has to show both in the upper and lower portions of the face. If the mouth 'smiles' by itself and the area around the eyes remains undisturbed, you may wonder whether the smile is real or fake. If you determine it to be fake, you need to assess whether or not your counterpart is also faking the emotion. You can often see the fake smiles in faces of politicians, salespeople, and entertainers.

An expression of happiness includes crow's feet around the eyes, with mouth and cheeks turning upward.

SADNESS

The emotion of sadness also involves muscles in the entire face. The corners of the mouth turn slightly downward. The eyes become unfocused, and in a severe emotional experience become watery. The upper eyelids slightly droop, and the eyebrows move together above the nose.

*Expressions of sadness include the mouth angling
downward, and drooping eyelids with the eyes losing focus.*

During a negotiation, the emotion of sadness usually occurs when the other side is disappointed. Make sure to understand why the disappointment exists. If left to simmer, it can
lead to your counterpart becoming discouraged and possibly
unable to cooperate further.

ANGER

An angry face expresses mainly in the mouth and eyes. The lips
press together, and the eyebrows move downward and closer
together. Often, wrinkles appear between the eyes above the
nose. The eyes focus on the other side, and glare.

Anger is an emotion that betrays the disconnecting of
synapses in the counterpart's brain. Anger needs to be

addressed quickly in a negotiation based on partnership before the frustration escalates into fury.

A display of anger includes lips pressed together, eyebrows down and together, and eyes glaring directly at the other side.

FEAR

A fearful face shows the lips stretched horizontally with the mouth slightly open. The eyebrows raise up, as well as the upper eyelids. The sclera around the pupil appears. Since we experience fear because we expect harm to come to us, this emotion also has a destructive effect on a partnership-oriented negotiation.

Fear starts with nervousness but can quickly devolve into desperation and panic. Your negotiation is over when that happens. Identify nervousness and dread quickly, and attempt to calm the counterparts if you want them to remain fully connected and open to negotiating.

Fear displays with the mouth extending sideways, eyebrows raised and pulled together, and raised upper eyelids.

SURPRISE

An open mouth, widened eyes, and raised eyebrows show surprise. This emotion is not necessarily negative. Surprise simply means that something unexpected happened. You now have to turn that surprise to your advantage. The other side has not prepared for whatever just happened, but hopefully, you have.

The element of surprise is a tool I use in most negotiations. It is a brief emotion, typically lasting only fractions of a second. If you notice the other side being surprised after a short pause, then it is likely a faked response. After the surprise passes, the other side will now assess whether the new information is positive or negative. Pay close attention to the secondary display of facial expressions after the surprise has passed.

*A look of surprise includes eyes wide open,
eyebrows raised, and the mouth slightly open.*

DISGUST

If something feels bad, tastes bad, or otherwise is offensive, we display disgust. The most obvious sign is the raising of only the upper lip and nose to create wrinkles at the top of the nose. The movement of the lip and nose upward also bares the teeth. If your counterpart reacts with disgust to your offer, it is definitely not a good offer to them.

You have to identify the source of disgust on the other side. Did an idea of yours arouse disgust, or the mentioning of a particular name? You can use the observation of disgust in your counterpart to identify serious personality conflicts. If mentioning a name that causes disgust for your counterpart, dislike at the minimum or revulsion at its worst, keep that particular person away from the negotiating table.

An expression of disgust includes the upper lip pulled up, nose wrinkled, and the upper teeth visible.

CONTEMPT

If you are watching your counterpart's face and you see one side of the mouth rising up, beware. A one-sided smile is not friendly. It is scornful. Contempt is a negative emotion and can destroy your negotiation if directed against you and left untreated.

Contempt shows that the other side feels superiority over you. The sense of superiority could derive from a social, moral, or professional background. You are in the lower quadrants on the sympathy and competence graph. It is time to work on both attributes; otherwise, an agreement is unlikely.

Displays of contempt and scorn include one side of the face tilting upward, while the other doesn't, and lips tightening slightly.

The most famous achievement of Paul Ekman is the identification of 'micro expressions'. Ekman noticed through his research that these seven basic emotions often appear as fleeting flashes on the face, not lasting longer than a fragment of a second. In my work as a trainer, I have captured many such micro-expressions on film and then played them back to my seminar participants.

There are additional emotional displays that I study a lot, as well. Shame, signaled by either looking down, maybe even covering the eyes, or pressing the mouth together while looking down or sideways, is an important emotion to notice. Why does a person experience shame? Are they lying? Do they have an inner conflict?

Another facial expression I am looking for is the pulling up of the chin with the lips pressing together. That is not anger. It is contentment. This expression usually is part of an internal dialog and shows acceptance of my facts. It is the precursor to an agreement.

A fleeting smile will signal whether an offer was good or bad, regardless if right afterward frustration or anger appear on the other side. It was a good offer, and now I will work on solidifying the agreement.

If I see contempt, a micro expression that occurs often, the offer certainly was not good. It may be time to reset your argumentation. It is the same with anger if I can notice it in a micro expression. Now I know I am facing resistance. I will have to work on the other side to make them recognize the win-win situation. All negative reactions, such as sadness, anger, disgust, or contempt will trigger in me the question of whether we need to take a break in order to get the other side fully connected again. Micro-expressions are a great tool to use for interpretation, but they require intense focus.

CHAPTER 22: Why Are You Blushing?

A teacher of mine once made a wise statement: All agreements are based on trust. He taught us MBA students that in business it does not matter what a contract spells out, and which clauses insure us against the other side failing to abide by the agreement. An agreement is paper. Trust and honesty are the bricks and mortar of any solid agreement.

With that in mind, lying is the most destructive force in cooperative professional interactions. The severity of lies has gradations, and therefore the damage could be anywhere from slight to catastrophic. Once lies have corrupted the line of arguments, clouded the assumptions, and raised the expectations, one outcome is virtually assured: Loss of trust. Professional relationships that are built upon a lack of trust, often the direct result of painful experiences of past betrayal and dishonesty, are, in my experience, short in scope and unprofitable in nature.

I believe in trust and honesty as the basis for business. Throughout my professional career I have fared well under this premise. I have formed strong bonds in my businesses, and have found that within the confines of honesty there is a lot of room for maneuvering smartly and pursuing the profit motive. Under this premise, making sure that the other side is telling me the truth is of utmost importance to me. Let me show you some of my tools for detecting if my counterpart is lying.

We have discussed stress management, verbal, and non-verbal communication in the previous chapters. We can form excellent methods for telling if someone is lying based upon these three pillars.

Usually, lying is stressful. I say 'usually' because there are habitual liars and sociopaths among us who do not feel any stress when lying. However, the large majority of people will display all the same stress symptoms when they lie that we discussed earlier in the book. The preparation for having to fight or flee causes increased blood pressure, pulse, breathing, and temperature. If you ask a pertinent question or you receive an important answer, watch the person across from you. The display of visible signals, such as blushing or paleness, sweating, tensing of muscles, stuttering, or increased breathing rate indicate stress related to the question or response in the verbal communication.

Non-verbal signals also manifest physical signs. The person that is lying will show signs of nervousness, such as adjusting their seating position. Zoology scientists discovered a phenomenon called 'displacement activity'. If you confront a rooster, for example, it might peck at some non-existing seeds rather than attack you. The reason is that the nervous system has not yet been able to decide on whether to fight or run away. So, a third, seemingly unrelated activity occurs. In human behavior, we are all familiar with these types of seemingly unrelated behaviors, like scratching your head if you are searching for an answer, or clicking the pen because you are nervous.

If someone is not telling the truth, there are specific displacement activities that can take place. Look for the person touching their nose or eyes. Elevated blood pressure under stress can cause an itching sensation in the small blood vessels of the nose. The pupils increase in size with increased blood pressure. Another theory is that quickly covering the mouth and the nose or rubbing one's eyes is an expression of trying to prevent the words from coming out, or blocking the image of a deceit.

People who are knowingly not telling the truth also engage in verbal activities that are not normal. Giving more information than necessary to answer a question is a tell-tale sign of deceit. A fake smile, where the mouth smiles but the eyes don't, while talking betrays stress and possible lying. Staring at the other side, not to make contact but to underscore trustworthiness, is a common sign of deceit, as well. In those cases, the verbal urge to convince the other side of the fact that they are not lying includes using words such as "believe me," "really," and "trust me."

People cannot play back a made-up experience. A real experience is like a movie in your memory. You can access it from all sides, play it forwards or backwards. Imagined experiences are more like static photographs in your memory. You line them up in a certain order when you imagine them. You will not be able to recall the pictures in a different order. FBI interrogators use this fact with suspects. They ask the suspect to describe a timeline, then ask the suspect to recall it backwards. If the timeline is a product of imagination, the suspect will have to reinvent a new series of pictures. The eyes will move to the imagination side of the brain.

Shame is an important emotion we may feel when we lie. How does shame manifest itself? We look down or away from the other side. We literally cannot 'face them'. We also often press the lips together and lower the edges of the mouth in a frown while we look down. Shame coincides with hanging shoulders, a posture of defeat, and a lowered head.

An expression of shame includes lips pressed together, and not meeting the eyes of the counterpart.

The eyes moving to the imagination side of the brain (top right for most) when making up an answer is a tell-tale sign. However, a word of caution: I have watched people telling a bold-faced lie while accessing the recall side of their brain. How did they do it? They recalled a situation that actually occurred, just not in the location or timeframe of the current conversation. Only if you pinpoint the portion of the answer that is imagined, will you be able to notice the eyes move to the imagination side of the brain.

"Was it on this Thursday that you called?" Bam!

The eyes look up and to the right for a visually constructed image.

Let me give you an example: In my lie detection trainings, I select two volunteers from the group of participants and give them a task. They have to leave the room and spend five minutes thinking about what they did the weekend before:

Friday night, Saturday, and Sunday. One of the two volunteers is supposed to answer truthfully when their colleagues ask them, but the other has to make up the entire weekend.

When they return to the training room, the remaining participants can ask them questions, one on one, sitting directly across from them. Watching the gestures, facial expressions, displays of stress, eye movements, and content of the answers, the participants then have to decide who of the two is the liar. I film the encounters with close-ups and mark instances when I see signals of lying or truth telling. To be fair to the group, I never inquire from the two volunteers who is the liar. So, I also do not know.

After all participants have had their turn at questioning, I show the video clips I made. The clips usually show eye movement, displays of stress, signs of discomfort, and other body language signaling deceit. I also document signals of honesty, trust, and self-assuredness. Now, I announce my decision. Then, I poll the room. Finally, the two volunteers tell us who lied and who didn't. Most of the time I am right. Sometimes, I am the lone accuser of one of the volunteers, while the rest of the class votes for the other volunteer as the liar. But, I admit, I have been wrong. One of the occasions when I was utterly wrong was when my volunteer was a professional poker player. He betrayed no stress and even managed to manipulate his eye movement. Another occasion was when the liar recalled a weekend that was not the previous weekend but a different one. Unless the pertinent question about the correct timing comes up, that person will access the recall side of the brain.

The good news is that most of us are not convincing liars. Make sure that you diligently ask the control questions early on in the negotiation. Then ask well-formulated questions about the pertinent issues of your negotiation. Closely observe the reactions of the other side. You almost always will be able to tell if someone is lying.

So, what do you do with that information? Can you still make an agreement? Should you? I guess it depends on the damage the lies can cause. I certainly will change my attitude towards the other side, make sure to safeguard the agreements we make, and immediately start looking for someone else with whom to do business. If a salesperson has lied to me, I have often in the past called their bosses with that information, and demanded their removal from my account. I don't work with liars.

CHAPTER 23: Last Pointers before Showtime

Okay, we are now ready to negotiate. We have identified all the tools, understand how to use them, and placed them into our negotiator's toolbox. As I warned in the beginning of this book, I spent the majority of our preparation time on the starting position. Once the data and facts are on the table, dependencies are clear, you have explored alternatives, and you have determined who the decision maker is, I spent a lot of time discussing the types of people we may encounter. What makes them tick? How might they react to my arguments? How do they decide? These are crucial questions that, if you can answer them in your preparation, will help you in the next step, the negotiation. Once you determine where you are, the next questions of where you want to be (goals), and how do you get there (strategies and tactics) are often obvious.

How important is preparation? My experience is that you can count on a very simple fact when negotiating with someone who is in a stronger bargaining position: They will not prepare well, because they are already confident of their victory. That has been an experience for me in the many tough negotiations I have conducted over the last dozen years. Good preparation reduces stress, builds confidence, and, most importantly, you are not relying on luck to win your negotiation.

Once you are well prepared and know who you are facing, you can use good question techniques and shine with quality small talk. You constantly observe, interpret, and react while negotiating. Here are some last pointers that I would like for you to internalize. I have noticed some mistakes that occur on a regular basis in my experience preparing and conducting hundreds of high-stakes negotiations.

Most common is a disconnect between strategy and tactics. This is especially prevalent in negotiations where emotions take over and turn a partnership strategy into pressure. Remember, take a break! Slow things down. If you are a Hunter, resist the itch to provoke a reaction from the other side. Not everyone takes this as a harmless jab, especially not the conflict-shy personalities, Scientists and Farmers.

Think through the entire negotiation. Prepare the negotiation room. It needs to be comfortable with enough space, and no distracting noise. You should serve something to drink, like coffee, tea, soft drinks, or water. If the rules allow it, also offer something to eat, like cookies, fruit, or even a sandwich around lunchtime. Serving nothing projects pressure!

Increase your small talk. If that portion of your negotiation is too short or not well done, it will project pressure or insecurity, bad preparation, and lack of empathy.

Don't interrupt the other side. After you ask an open-ended question, let the other side talk. Let them articulate their 'teddy bear', their goals, and their idea of a win-win situation. Remember, interruption is a pressure tactic that throws the other side off their game.

Listen more than you talk. Remember the 80/20 rule. Ask good questions, but also give the other side time to present their case. Engaging in monologues might feel good to you, but remember, you want to know what kind of pizza the other side likes. At this point, whatever pizza you like is not relevant.

Don't box yourself in with time limits. Figuring out a win-win situation takes extra time. Looking on your watch or announcing that you have another meeting in fifteen minutes is pressure, not partnership. If you really have another meeting that can't be moved, then postpone the negotiation for when you have the time to devote to it.

Don't forget about the first impression. You are setting the tone for the entire meeting in the first few minutes. Be welcoming, maybe even show respect by having reserved a special parking spot or introducing your boss. Smile when you greet your counterpart. If they are nervous, put them at ease. Do not allow them to cut the small talk short or somehow speed up the meeting. Keep your pace. It is your negotiation, not theirs.

Remember, if you've selected a partnership strategy it is because of your evaluation of the starting position and your goals. It does not matter whatsoever if the other side chose a pressure strategy and is pursuing it. If you are goaded into leaving your side of the field and playing on the other side's turf, you've just thrown out all of your preparation and have given the other side all the advantage. If the other side uses pressure against me, I think of it as a game. The challenge is to see how good I really am in de-escalating, and killing aggression with smiles, objectivity, and facts. Believe me, it feels rewarding when the other side raises the white flag and comes over on your turf. You should try it.

Don't justify to yourself that you went to pressure in the middle of a negotiation because it was your strategic choice. Be honest with yourself. If you had not prepared a partnership leading to pressure strategy and had not defined clear decision points for the switch, you have just allowed the other side to pull you over onto their turf. Several important lightbulbs probably went dark and you gave in to one of Ekman's seven basic emotions, anger. File it away as a learning experience when that happens. And it happens to all of us. Debrief yourself and your negotiation partners after a negotiation, accept the lesson, and steel yourself for the next time. Power is not in using pressure. Power is in the success of your approach, especially if you are facing tough odds.

One of the biggest mistakes I see is a lack of observation. If you make an offer, you have to look at the other side. A movie is playing, and you are supposed to watch it. Conversely, if you receive an offer and you don't want to betray your thinking and feeling, look down, take notes, even doodle if you don't want to write anything down. That way the other side cannot see your facial expression.

Make your offers simple, and learn them by heart. Offers that are so complicated that you have to read them should be prepared in advance. Use a flip chart and an easel, write your offer on the second page and cover it. When the right moment arrives, get up, unveil your offer, and observe your counterparts. If you have a negotiation partner, let him or her write the offer on a white board or flip chart. Our sensory system is wired to look where something is happening. Teach yourself that what is happening is the reaction of your counterparts, not in your partner's beautiful handwriting. Never, ever watch your partner. Always look at the other side. Observe, analyze, react!

While we are talking about the whiteboard or flip chart, write down intermediate results for everyone to see. This is the easiest way to prevent a misunderstanding. Write down what the other side has just agreed to. Once it is on the board, they can dispute it. If they don't, it stays even if the meeting discontinues for some reason. I have been in negotiations in Asia, where we wrote intermediate results on a board, and asked our counterparts to sign the board. Then, we took a picture of the signed whiteboard, which we distributed to all participants of the meeting.

Give feedback in a way that is not accusatory. Tell your counterparts how something makes you feel, not what they did to you. Remember, your perception of reality is not necessarily their perception of reality. Accept the possibility that the other side might not have intended to do something. The proper feedback will allow them to rebalance the situation. Keep in mind what type of personality you are facing. Look behind the façade. Understand where they are coming from, what motivates them, and how they view the situation. Be open, and look for clues so you understand them better.

And one more thing, for Goodness' Sake, ask open-ended questions! Ask, ask, and you shall receive. It is one of the simplest tools I have provided, and it also will be one of the most productive you have in your arsenal. I have observed negotiations as a coach during which I internally screamed at my negotiators to just ask some questions. I could see their counterparts itching to speak. We just ignored them.

Who are the best negotiators around, you may ask? No, neither you nor me. Children are the best negotiators. Observe them when you have the opportunity. Children have pronounced body language, unspoiled from the pressures of grown-up life. Children also have not yet developed effective defensive strategies, such as hiding dishonesty or putting a façade over their personality preferences. I can confidently say that my sons have taught me a lot over the years. Here is a little story to illustrate:

One winter evening, around 8:00 at night, I was sitting in the living room of our house in rural Virginia. My wife tended to our baby in the kid's room upstairs. My four-year-old son sat on my lap while I was reading him a story. It was one of Grimm's fairy tales, and he was mesmerized. "Then the witch died," I concluded, "and the moral of the story…" My wife called down from the upstairs bedroom.

"It's eight o'clock," she shouted. "Fabian has to go to bed." Before I could make the first move to get up, Fabian grabbed my cheeks with his little hands.

"Papi," he said, "you are the best Papi in the whole wide world!" He gave me a kiss. "I love you!" My heart was melting. He continued: "Papi, will you read me one more story?" Pressure or partnership? It was a diabolical combination of both. Was my brain fully connected? No. Was this communication from the Free Child? Absolutely! Needless to say, of course I read another story… perhaps two.

I put together some real-life cases for you in the final part of the book from my years as a negotiator. I split the cases by providing a starting position and, after giving you the chance to think about each case, then giving you the rest of the story. I wish you the best of luck in your upcoming negotiations. Perhaps we may meet one of these days in a seminar or at the table in a negotiation!

PART 4: Cases

This section contains actual cases. I have masked the names of people and companies in order to protect them and myself. I have also recreated the conversations as I remembered them, or as I was told. So, take these cases for what they are: The opportunity to study the tools we discussed in the previous chapters in action. Not every negotiation requires every tool, but the larger the toolbox and the better equipped you are, the more options you have for success.

For each case, I describe a large portion of the starting position, sometimes the goals, as well. Then, I have a page break. Take the time to internalize the information. Use the preparation worksheet below and think through your options: Where am I? Where do I want to be? How do I get there?

I will tell you what actually transpired in 'The Rest of the Story'. That does not mean I present the only option. Since I showed you how resourceful I can be in the previous parts, I am sure you don't mind that I purposely show you cases that have had a good outcome. Have fun...

Preparation Worksheet

Your Own Team:	The Opposing Team:
Starting Position:	**Starting Position:**
Alternatives?	Alternatives?
Dependencies?	Dependencies?
Who is Coming?	Who is Coming?
❏ Scientist	❏ Scientist
❏ Farmer	❏ Farmer
❏ Merchant	❏ Merchant
❏ Hunter	❏ Hunter
❏ Decision Maker	❏ Decision Maker
Goals:	**Goals:**
❏ Maximum	❏ Maximum
❏ Minimum	❏ Minimum
❏ Worst Case	❏ Worst Case
Strategy	**Strategy**
❏ Pressure Tactics	❏ Pressure Tactics
❏ Partnership Tactics	❏ Partnership Tactics
Items to be confirmed:	**Items to be confirmed:**

Figure 15: Preparation Worksheet

Case #1

I once coached a sourcing case that offered absolutely no opportunity to achieve a good result. And... it had to do with a monopolist supplier, as you can probably imagine. In this case, the development supplier of a large OEM helped develop a gearbox for an all-wheel-drive sedan. The little device sat next to the main transmission. The supplier had been extremely helpful, supplied lots of design ideas and testing services. When the car went into production, the part worked flawlessly, and its price was within the budget. However, soon after that the demeanor of the supplier changed rapidly. Gone was the friendly, cooperative spirit. Demands started to inundate the Purchasing Department with engineering change orders, additional tooling cost, and logistics expenses for delivery racks.

After the first year of production, and despite a firm contract for five years with annual "productivity" savings, the supplier demanded a ten percent price increase rather than passing on the agreed to three percent discount. The buyers and purchasing managers on the case immediately threatened to cancel the contract, find the part elsewhere, and even sue the supplier. All for naught. A ten percent price increase it became.

Management was furious. It became clear in meetings with Engineering that there was no option to change suppliers. The part in question had a shape unlike any other comparable supplier's product, and Engineering had shaped the chassis to accommodate. The next makeover of the car was not on the schedule for another four years. Changing the chassis in mid-production was next to impossible. Changing the part in that timeframe was even further from reality. The supplier, well aware of their bargaining power, submitted another increase of eight percent for the following year. Now the place was on fire! I was asked to help prepare this upcoming negotiation.

We looked under every stone for a solution during the brainstorming sessions with the purchasing team, including a senior manager. Could we offer deals on new projects? Could we bundle the part with other parts the supplier made? Nothing.

Here are some key pieces of information I found in my research:

1) The head of the OEM's Engineering Department had just started with the company three months ago.
2) The supplier had a resident engineer in their Engineering Department.
3) The salesman relied heavily on my customer for his commissions.
4) Senior management was adamant to try anything to break the cycle of the supplier's blackmail.

Take a moment to think about this case. Any ideas?

Here is the rest of the story:
The Chassis Fake

I threw the only viable idea out for discussion: Fake the redesign of the chassis. The manager chuckled. I observed embarrassed downward gazes from the buyers. *Did I not know that that was impossible? The supplier would never believe it.* Once a car is in production, basic changes such as this have huge costs and risks associated with them. It is simply not done. "Okay," I responded, "any better ideas?" I asked for two weeks and a free hand in the negotiation. The manager agreed.

I had researched the Engineering Department. Clearly, someone had an awfully close relationship with this supplier. After all, the spec had been written so that no other part would fit into the chassis. Even worse, the supplier had a resident engineer working on the same floor with all the other engineers. This did not bode well for keeping a realistic fake alive. Who could we trust to support this outrageous fake? I decided to approach the Vice President of Engineering, a lady who had taken over the department less than three months before. She was the first woman to ever run this part of the company. This project had remarkably high visibility. Maybe this was an opportunity to impress senior management with her skills.

She, like everyone else in the company, knew about the problem with this supplier. I asked her for complete secrecy. Then I told her my plan...

That Friday, Karen called a staff meeting. The apparent purpose was to talk about future projects, a new SUV was on the horizon. At the end of the meeting, she asked two engineers to stay behind. The rest of the staff left the room wondering what that was all about. An hour later, the two engineers packed up their desks and computers. They moved into a room down the hall with extra security reserved for extremely sensitive developments. When colleagues asked, they could only say that they were working on a redesign project. The rumor in the department was that they redesigned the chassis of the all-wheel-drive sedan. The supplier's resident engineer heard it too...

Tuesday morning the phone rang at my buyer's desk in the Purchasing Department. "Hey, how are you?" the supplier salesman inquired in a saccharine voice.

"Fine, what's up?" the buyer responded.

"Well, just wanted to see how things are going. I know there is some friction here. What can I do to help? Should I come by? We can talk about it."

I had told the buyer to play it cool—no threats—only to hint that the supplier's brinkmanship might backfire.

"If you want to help, then send me an offer with a twenty percent discount, which is what your contract specifies," the buyer said calmly. "You know, senior management is on the case now. When you sent in for another eight percent increase, you created a mess. I wouldn't want you to be seen around here under these circumstances," he added

After a quick pause, the salesman answered, "You know I can't do that! We have much higher costs now. Blah, blah, blah..." The conversation ended.

Wednesday afternoon the salesman called again. "Hey, Joey, I talked to my boss. He thinks it would be a good idea for him and me to meet with your manager. We don't want this to escalate."

Joey, the buyer, shot back, "No way do we want to see you or your boss unless you have a twenty percent discount on a piece of paper with your logo on it. Don't even think that you can show up here."

We had planned on organizing a meeting between us and the sales manager to set up a good guy/bad guy scenario. The supplier made it easy. Thursday morning, the sales manager called our purchasing manager and said that he had an offer that he wanted to discuss directly with him. Our manager set the meeting for Friday morning, 9:00 AM.

We decided that the manager would get the sales manager and his salesman into a small, uncomfortable meeting room. The offer we expected might be that they dropped their current eight percent demand. If that was the case, we already had an acceptable result, but we really wanted to undo the previous year's price increase. The purchasing manager was to reject the offer outright, physically tear the sheet into little pieces, and storm out of the room red-faced. The buyer and I were to stay behind and make sure the offer would not be retracted.

Friday morning came. We met the sales manager, a young, dapper, immaculately dressed, take-no-prisoners type. The salesman—I had only seen a photo on LinkedIn—was in his 50s with gray hair, long over the ears and collar. He looked pale and unhealthy, wearing an ill-fitting suit, slightly overweight, and clearly not comfortable in the situation. We were nice enough, exchanged a few pleasantries, but made no bones about the fact that this was serious. We did not serve anything. Our manager came in five minutes late deliberately, refused to shake hands, sat down, and looked at the sales manager.

"What do you have for me?" he asked bluntly.

The sales manager did not miss a beat. He started talking about the long and productive relationship and went on and on. Our manager cut him off.

"I have to be in another meeting in four minutes. What is your offer? It'd better be a good one."

"We are dropping our price increase for this year," the sales manager announced, looking for a hurray and smiles on the other side. No such luck.

"What?" our manager exclaimed. "No discount? Are you guys deaf? We want a twenty percent discount, not a penny less!"

He abruptly jumped up and headed for the door.

"Goodbye, Gentlemen," he huffed, and slammed the door behind him.

There was awkward silence. I looked at the sales manager, then at the salesman. They were in shock.

"He is pretty pissed," I said.

The buyer nodded. The salesman shifted uncomfortably on his chair.

"He's usually a really nice guy. But this…" I added.

"We really value the relationship with you. This is a really good offer," the salesman chirped.

Was this a peace offering?

"It is not an offer at all," Joey said calmly. "If you want to save this relationship, you need to come up with a discount. We would be due the second three percent productivity this coming year. That makes six percent plus the 10% you stuck us with last year. Anything less than that will be unacceptable."

The sales manager got up. "We will see what we can do. I will get back with you after the weekend."

We shook hands with friendly smiles and Joey escorted them out. The salesman slumped over, looking broken when they left. But I had a good feeling about this. The sales manager kept his poker face. Still, our fake seemed to be working. Even though it was unlikely that we actually were redesigning the chassis, we had them wondering...

The weekend came and went. Monday, we received no messages. Tuesday went by. We were sitting on eggshells. *No, we will not call!* Finally, Wednesday late morning the phone rang. The salesman was calling Joey.

"Joey, we need another meeting. My manager thinks this was a big misunderstanding."

Joey quickly shot back, "No discount, no meeting! Send us what you've got, and I will take it to my manager."

"We are finalizing an offer. Obviously, this is way over my head. Can my manager talk directly to your manager?"

"You want him to talk to my manager? Don't think so. He does not want to waste another minute on this. Are you aware of the waves you've created here?" Joey asked. "This goes all the way up to the top. I would fix this quickly if I were you."

"I will have something tomorrow," the salesman promised, and hung up.

I had two days left before my two-week time on this experiment was up.

Thursday, 4:00 PM Joey came into the conference room, where I led a working session for some buyers. He had a piece of paper in his hand. "Here it is!"

He handed it to me. The supplier offered to give a 10% discount. This beat all our expectations.

I took Joey aside. "This is good," I said. "Try one more thing. Tell the supplier that we need a binding commitment for three percent over the next three years. Then, we'll be ready to take the offer to our management."

We closed the deal Friday morning. Ten percent now, zero percent Year Two, three percent Year Three, and three percent Year Four. We had almost gotten back to the original contract!

The two engineers packed up their computers that afternoon and moved back to their old desks. They had never been told that they were working on a fake. The supplier believes to this day that they almost lost us, and that we were redesigning the chassis. Nobody lied, either.

The key to this case was the cooperation between the Engineering manager and the Purchasing Department. Withholding information from the engineers churned the rumor mill. While a resident engineer usually provides intelligence to sales, in this case that intelligence was misinformation. Don't try this at home!

Key Concepts and Factors that Helped Win this Case
- Starting position
- Communication and relationships
- Using Avoidance strategy, then Pressure
- Faking an Alternative

CASE #2

A few years ago, I conducted a management training session for one of my favorite OEM clients. The Director of Purchasing who sponsored the management training for his department, and who participated himself, was highly respected. He was tough but fair, and open-minded. We had known each other for a few years. Over lunch, he put me on the spot in front of all of his managers.

"What would you do with this, Harry?" He started out. "We have a warehouse just across the street here. If we could buy it, we could close the street and increase our campus significantly."

The background is that this particular production facility was old. Pre-World War II old. It used to be on the edge of town, but over the decades, the town had grown up around it. A railroad track formed the border of the campus on one side, and a residential area on the other. The only place for expansion was on the third side, where the OEM already had purchased land and built administrative buildings. A public road bisected this section of the administrative buildings and the manufacturing side. Next to these administrative buildings stood a warehouse with a large parking area. The owner of that warehouse used to be a supplier, but his business had folded about a decade ago. In the meantime, he had started a small business that required tractor trailers to drive in and out of the property. The business only occupied a small portion of the building. The OEM had tried for years to buy the building from the owner, but to no avail. He did not want to sell. So, the OEM had rented most of the building. Now the lease was up.

George Sweeney, the Purchasing Director, looked me straight in the face. "What would you do?" Of course, without much knowledge of the case, I asked him how old the owner was. In his seventies, was the answer.

I looked at the director. "Does he have children? Do you know them?"

"Why do you need to know?" George shot back.

I said, "Well, what if his children actually don't agree with the old man. Maybe they want him to sell. Then, you have natural allies. They could help your negotiation."

He smiled. "Interesting thought," he mumbled. I had passed the test.

Each time I visited the OEM to conduct trainings over the following year, I asked the Director how his negotiation was going. He remained vague.

Then one day, I received the call I was expecting. "Harry, we need you to help us buy that damn warehouse."

And off I went to the airport.

The details I discovered about the case were the following:

1) The owner of the building indeed was 70 years old. His business had gone bankrupt about ten years earlier. The new business was small but expanding. The warehouse was not suited for this type of business.

2) The owner had been a premier league football quarterback in his twenties. He was nationally known. He now lived quite far away in a nice house on the beach, and spent most of his days playing golf.

3) The OEM had tried to shut down half the access road leading to the warehouse. The city turned down the application after emphatic protests from the warehouse owner. The road constriction would have shut down his small business since tractor trailers could not turn into the property anymore.

4) The OEM had organized a meeting several years before, during which six members of the Purchasing Department

confronted the warehouse owner, who was by himself, and tried to force him to sell by using all manner of threats.

5) The OEM had invested significantly in building modifications to house their production. That investment would be lost—but even worse—the OEM never asked the owner for permission! The owner could theoretically charge for restoring the building to pre-lease conditions.

6) The lease with the warehouse owner expired three months later and was written in such a way that the OEM could be expelled, literally, the next day.

Take a moment to think about this case. Any ideas?

Just be Nice!
Here is the rest of the story:

That was a tough one. We were under tremendous time pressure since the lease would expire three months later. The warehouse owner had no reason to cooperate. After all, we had pressured him, even threatened his livelihood when we tried to shut down the road. But...

Casting all emotions aside, I started thinking about this man: A football star and a successful businessman whose last venture turned into a bankruptcy. I also learned from researching his business online, that his wife owned the current business and, most likely, the umbrella company that managed the warehouse, as well. He was retired, played golf all day, and lived in a nice house on the beach. Why in the world would anyone want to drag around an old warehouse that did not even suit their small business? If I were the warehouse owner, I would take the cash and walk. Play more golf, enjoy retirement.

I asked people in the department that had met the owner what he was he like. One buyer said that he thought he was a nice guy, that his employees liked him, and that before all the friction with him, he was always friendly and cooperative. The Purchasing Director, who had also met him and tried to pressure him into a sale, thought that he was stubborn, emotional, and not at all cooperative. The warehouse owner had literally stormed out of the office during their last meeting.

What type of personality might this man be, I wondered? Clearly, he reacted badly to pressure. His synapses had disconnected, he got mad, and had even stormed out of a prior meeting. Otherwise, when fully connected, he was nice and cooperative. Also, the golf and beach mansion suggested a prestigious lifestyle. A football quarterback clearly was a Hunter-type role. A Hunter without power was my impression. His business had failed, and his wife owned the assets. He fought under pressure, no matter the consequences or the objective advantage of a settlement.

How do you deal with a Hunter? YOU DON'T USE PRESSURE! But that is what had happened. Now the trust was broken. The warehouse owner had lost face, especially in front of his wife. That was reason enough not to agree to a deal. So, how to reset the negotiation?

Step 1: Replace the negotiators. Personality conflict and grudges have no place in a negotiation. I asked the Purchasing Director to allow me to work with one of his best managers as a negotiation partner, and to let me negotiate directly in an assumed role: A neutral role. I decided to take the role of a corporate real estate specialist from the home office in another country. That gave me authority, but also emotional distance.

Step 2: What was my starting position? We had already gone through all kinds of details. But I wondered if there was a dependency on the other side. We were highly dependent. The owner could expel us in three months when the lease was up. We would not only lose the chance to buy the building, but also the significant investment we had made. But was the owner dependent on us? I thought he was. Who would lease this building other than us? As a Purchasing Department we could tell all our suppliers that they would lose us as a customer if they rented the building. I had a great argument for that: We didn't need competition for wages three steps from our production facility. Makes sense, doesn't it? Of course, that was a pressure tactic, but what were his plans for leasing the building to someone else? So far, we knew no one else had looked at the building. It would take at least a year to find a new tenant, and the lease per square foot would be low because it was an old building. The landlord would have to invest in improvements, which could not be good for him. I decided that he really wanted to at least continue the lease. So did we.

Step 3: If we chose partnership as the strategy, what was the teddy bear? Clearly, we had to create a win-win situation for the owner. The budget for the purchase of the warehouse was low. I managed at least to get the director to agree to the current real estate market price for a warehouse that size, but he really wanted to spend less. What else could we offer? I had called real estate brokers throughout the entire region to get a feel for what type of buildings were available. I also researched the owner's business and figured out what kind of building was better suited. What if we offered a straight swap? He would get a new building outside of town and closer to the freeways that was better suited for his expanding business. And we would take his building, close the road and increase our campus. Does it not sound like a great win-win? I got to work on that option. My main problem, it turned out, was that the buildings I found were way more expensive than what we wanted to pay for this building.

Step 4: Tactics. I asked the Purchasing Director for two specific things: First, I wanted him to be out-of-town and give us his office to conduct the negotiation. That gave us a physical proof of having decision-making power, the boss' office. And with the boss out of town, there was no chance for the owner to insist on talking to the Director rather than negotiating with us. Second, I wanted to set the appointment between 12:00 and 1:00 PM and offer a catered lunch. Oh, my goodness, I could have asked for anything! But providing lunch to a supplier, especially this guy... The director bristled. As a firm rule, this

OEM never offered anything other than water to a supplier. I offered to pay for it myself if I had to. I got the lunch.

It was the day of the negotiation. I had never met the owner before, so all my assumptions were probability-based. I had to verify them as quickly as possible. My negotiation partner, Andy, picked Mr. Owens up from the reception.

When Owens approached me, he shook my hand firmly, looked around, and said, "Where is George [the Purchasing Director]?" He was direct, down to the point. Indication: Hunter.

I motioned to the little conference table with the catered food. "He is out of town today, but I will run the meeting."

"Who are you?" he asked, not sitting down. "You have a German accent."

Yep, more Hunter.

"And who is your partner-in-crime, here?" he added.

"I am from the corporate office in charge of real estate. And, yes, I am German. My colleague manages general purchases here." I handed him my business card.

"Germans. Dealt with a lot of them. Good engineers. Kicked their asses seventy years ago. Where did you learn English?"

No offense intended. He was just a typical Hunter.

"I studied in the US," I replied.

"It's pretty good."

That was a compliment, coming from a Hunter. He sat down. I offered him something to drink, and he accepted. But he was not hungry. I hoped George would never hear about that.

"So," Owens immediately cut to the chase, "you want to talk about my building."

I grabbed a sandwich and leaned back. "Before we start, Mr. Owens, I would like to ask you a question."

He looked at me. "Shoot," he said.

"I have never met a football star before. You are famous. What a career! Do you still have any connections to your team?"

"Well, that was a long time ago," he smiled, clearly pleased with the accolades. "I haven't played football in 45 years. These days, I play golf."

He leaned back, signaling open body language. I was getting somewhere.

"You play golf? You know, I have never played on a team at your level. I grew up with soccer. My favorite position in my village team was goalie. That way, I didn't have to run so much."

He laughed. "I have a lot of respect for goalies. They are the last line of defense. I used to hit them with all I had."

"I can only imagine," I picked up the line. "I had some balls hit me straight in the face. I got more than one bloody nose-- even a broken collarbone once."

"Ouch," he grimaced. He leaned forward, clearly done with the small talk.

"Okay, this is not why I am here," Owens said, keeping me on task. "You guys suck!" he exclaimed.

Now that almost triggered an 'Ouch!' from me. I kicked my partner under the table and gave him a look that said, *Don't take the bait!*

"You guys tried to close the road to my place. I heard about it through the newspaper."

"Through the newspaper, really? That is awful," I empathized. "When was that? I just got here, so I don't know much about the history here. Tell me more."

"George, your boss here," he pointed at the empty desk, "tried to bully me. Six guys sitting across from me. Hey, but," he thumped his chest, "didn't work with this old warhorse."

"Six guys against one!" I smiled at him. "Well, we know you know how to take on the big guys," I said, referencing his football background. "You and I know that you are a tough cookie. Hell, I would be too scared to take you head on," I added.

His chest expanded. "You better believe it!"

This game went on for twenty minutes. He spewed out every misgiving he had about our company, our relationship, the previous negotiations, the late rent payments, and, of course, the fact that we had modified his building without asking permission.

I just took it all in. I made a few comments showing disbelief and sympathy. Then, finally, he was done.

"So, what do you want?" he asked me. "You know, your lease is up." Here it was.

I had set myself two goals: One, to try to expand the lease for another year at the old price In the best case, and go up to thirty percent higher if we had to. That would give us some breathing room. The second was to buy the building at, or below, market price. The swap was my least preferred option because the new building was too expensive for us.

"The lease is up," I agreed.

"I am not sure what we're going to do," I replied.

"But what are you going to do with the space?" I looked him straight in the eyes.

I waited ten seconds.

He was thinking.

"Hmmm," he said, pushing the edges of his mouth down and crinkling his chin.

"We would be interested in extending the lease." I poked.

A fleeting smile rushed across his face, an indication that he liked the offer.

"I would be fine with that. Same price?" he asked.

Okay, I thought, he does not have another option for the building. He did not want to risk that we might actually leave. I decided to secure this lease right now and not risk anything by trying to get the price down. The current lease cost was our maximum goal—and we had prepared to pay up to thirty percent more.

"That would be fine," I responded. "One year, no more," I added. He looked at me with disappointment.

"I thought, we might be able to do something more long term," Owens said.

"You are looking for predictability and security? Let's revisit that later," I closed the discussion, but left the prospect of addressing his fears open.

I wrote down, 'Lease extension for one year at current rate.' I pushed the paper across for him to look at. He nodded.

"That's right," he said.

Okay. First goal achieved. I also knew that if we could not come to an agreement on buying the building, we could then revisit the lease cost and get a discount for a two-year agreement.

"I have a proposal for you," I started the next part of the discussion.

Mr. Owens leaned forward, obviously interested to hear what I was bringing to the table.

"What if we had a building, same size as yours, in the industrial park outside of town? It's located right next to the freeway. Wide access. Rail terminal a few miles down the road. What if we swap? You take that building; we take yours here?"

I let the proposal linger. He rubbed his chin (contemplation).

"I had not thought of this idea before," he admitted.

I smiled. Surprise is good. I watched him closely as he digested the idea.

"You have the building already?" he asked. Good move. He got me.

"We have access to it," I diverted. "It is no problem for us. As you know, we operate warehouses in the industrial area, so do several of our suppliers."

I added, "You know, we don't like our suppliers to have operations too close to the factory. We don't want to compete for labor."

If he had planned to use the prospect of new renters connected to us, I wanted to shut the possibility down. It was similar to snipers taking position on the roofs around the bank. No one is getting killed in the current scenario, but don't try to leave the building if you are the bank robber.

I left it at that. A cloud of disappointment washed across his face. He looked down. He knew what I had just said. I kept silent.

"It is an intriguing idea," he finally admitted. "But I thought you wanted to buy my building outright?"

Ahah! He wanted the money! He wanted retirement. He wanted golf. He wanted the beach house. He wanted his wife off his back. Okay.

"Buy the building outright? Well, yes, we do," I looked at him like a son might look at his dad. "You never wanted to sell it. Besides, this is an old building. We would probably tear it down and build something else in its place. You know our company. We can't pay more than it is worth to us."

Slightly agitated, he leaned forward.

"It is worth every penny," he insisted. "Especially, given where it is located."

"It is actually not in a great spot, as you know," I countered quickly. "It is hard to access."

"Well for me it is," he leaned back. "For you it is in the middle of your campus." He seemed worried that we would not make an offer.

"Like I said," I continued, "we can only pay…" I threw out a really low number, about half of what the market price for a building like that would be.

I watched his reaction closely. He did not show any signs of anger or disappointment. Hmmm. Good offer? I wondered.

"That is ridiculous," he finally shot across the table. *Too late,* I thought. That was not his genuine reaction. I kept playing the low number.

I had an idea. A Hunter always wants to save face. Owens wanted to come home to his wife with a trophy. This was it:

"It seems difficult for you to agree. What if we sweeten the deal?" I asked.

He was clearly interested.

"We agree on the purchase price," I continued. We also agree on a one-year lease at the current rate. Upon signing the agreement, we will pay you a cash down-payment of …"

He smiled. Good offer.

After another half-an-hour of going back and forth, we reached an agreement. We had the lease extended for one year at the current rate. We committed to paying a certain amount as non-refundable earnest money for the option to buy the building after twelve months—for a fraction of the market value that I had established.

It was a sweet deal. Mr. Owens was happy, as well, and felt that he had made a good deal. He had been worried that we let him get stuck with the building without renewing the lease. What we also did not know was that he had already sold his share in the small business that he had in the building. He was off to the beach and golf course for good in a well-deserved retirement.

Turns out Owens was a nice man, but definitely a Hunter without power. Once he had spewed out all the misgivings from the last few years of dealing with the OEM, he was willing to make a deal that was fair. The key to this negotiation was twofold: Always test your assumptions and ask lots of questions. Open questions. Also learn to dial back your ego. Owens wanted to save face. He wanted to be respected and get some satisfaction for the bad treatment he perceived to have received. So, we let him. The result counts!

Key Concepts and Factors that Helped Win this Case:
- Starting position
- Preparing the negotiation space and atmosphere
- Recognizing The Hunter personality, especially allowing the other side to save face
- Dialing back one's ego
- Asking good questions
- Quality small talk
- Partnership strategy and tactics

CASE #3

One of my earliest experiences in professional negotiations dates back to my twenties. I had met my wife, and when she became pregnant with our first son, I decided to quit my history PhD studies and look for a more lucrative career. Not too long after that, I found a job at the largest polyester yarn manufacturer in the world.

The first year as a management trainee was tough. I spent months in the factories, learning to thread yarn into these huge, scary texturing machines. Then, I came back to harvest the full packages, as yarn rolls were called. These packages spun at a speed of 600 to 700 rounds per minute. The machines never stopped, so I had to open the cradle, put my bare hand underneath the package, let it drop into my hand, and let it spin out. Yes, your read correctly: In my bare hand! You can just imagine that these hands of an historian, educator, and researcher had no callouses to mitigate dealing with intense friction and heat. To the great amusement of my co-workers, but not so much to my shift supervisors, I had dropped many of these yarn packages onto the floor, from whence they rolled hundreds of feet down the 200,000 square-foot factory.

But... I am tough. And determined. And proud. I learned to do this. I also learned lots of other things, especially the logic of how to assemble information from different machines in different parts of the manufacturing process into usable management tools. That was right up a trained historian's alley. Within six months of working as a management trainee, the Industrial Engineering Department rescued me from the factory floor. And within a month of working there, doing time studies with a stopwatch to check how long people took to go to the bathroom and other mind-numbing tasks, I redesigned the operations of the Traffic Department. All of our yarn was shipped out from there, and all raw materials came into that location. It was complicated, and totally new. I had fun.

That fun did not last too long, however. After a six-month stint as a Traffic Department manager, higher-ups thought that I needed to be in sales. A position had just opened in Europe for a Market Development Manager, and I was chosen to fill it. While working in Logistics, I had also just started on an Executive MBA program and bought a house. Our child was two years old. Welcome to corporate life! Within two weeks, I was sitting in my new office in Birmingham, UK. My wife was lagging a few weeks behind, tasked with packing up and selling the house. Finally, she arrived with child and dog in tow, one of whom had to go into the mandatory six-month Customs quarantine.

My new boss was an interesting guy. He was not much older than me, born and raised in Northern Ireland. He had lived several years in France and spoke French fluently. Now he headed sales in all of Europe for our company. Most of the yarn for the European market came from a factory in Ireland, just across the border from Londonderry, or Derry, depending on where you came from. At that time, Northern Ireland was in the throes of a brutal, and bloody, civil war.

My boss, Marmaduke Manson, had grown up in this mess. Consequently, he was highly opinionated and full of prejudice. There was not a country in Europe, for which he could not find a choice derogatory description—except France, of course. I, a German, raised Catholic, represented pretty much the sum of all his prejudice. It follows that the countries I had in my portfolio also attracted the object of his ire: Lithuania, Poland, Czech Republic, Slovakia, Hungary, Rumania, Austria, Switzerland, and Italy. Italy came into my portfolio, not because it was a developing market for our company, but because my boss hated Italians. He did not want anything to do with them, and they certainly returned the sentiment. Despite this awkward situation, our sales in Italy were growing. And I love Italy…

One morning, about three weeks after I started my new job, and still trying to figure out what was expected of me, Manson came into my office.

"Harry," he said. "We have an emergency."

I perked up from staring at my computer screen. 'Emergency'? That sounded interesting.

"Tessitura Tessuto Mancietti just had a complete shut-down." He said.

Really? Wow! Mancietti was the largest weaver in Italy.

"Did they go bankrupt?" I asked.

"I wish," Manson replied. "I really wish."

"What happened?" I asked

"We happened," he replied.

Apparently, our company had shipped bad yarn to this weaver. It shut down the plant. This was huge. Basically, there are two types of yarn in weaving. The yarn that runs the full length of a fabric is called the warp yarn. It has to be top quality. A difference in tension or texture could create a variance in the dying process. The entire fabric, up to a mile long, could be ruined. The other type of yarn, the weft, was not as critical when it came to quality. Weft yarn shoots from one side through the loom to the other. If the weft yarn does not dye well, only that small portion of fabric is cut out. But as it turned out, our quality defect appeared in the warp yarn.

"You need to go there," Manson instructed me sternly. "I need two things: We have to retain the customer, and I want you to minimize the claim."

According to Manson, Mr. Mancietti had already called and threatened him with $4,000 per hour penalties for his looms sitting idle. That amounted to $96,000 per day. We had just entered Day Four. I asked Manson if I had anything to offer the customer.

"We have six trucks loaded with replacement product at the factory [in Ireland]. It will replace all of his bad yarn. As soon as you make a deal, we can send them down there," he promised.

Take a few minutes and think about this case. How would you set your goals? What is your worst case?

Ambiguous Goals
Here is the rest of the story:

It was 9:00 AM. I called our Travel Department, reserved a ticket, and departed for the airport.

I arrived at Malpensa Airport in Milano three hours later, hailed a cab, and was in Mancietti's office by 1:00 PM. He was livid. He screamed at me from the top of his lungs. In addition, his desk stood on a one-foot riser, and I sat on a sofa in front. He towered over me, gesticulating madly, and making his displeasure unmistakably known.

"You ruined my company," he screamed. "My family, my children—all ruined."

I said nothing.

He pointed his index finger at me.

"You... I can find your family," he threatened. "I can make your life hell."

And on, and on, and on. I love Italy and I love Italians. I find that Mediterranean peoples can get emotional and their reactions can be over the top. Mancietti definitely was that day.

It was not difficult for me to remain calm. Other than having to fear for my life and that of my family for the rest of time, it was like being an extra in a B-rated movie. Just a year-and-a-half earlier, I had been researching my dissertation, engaged in intellectually challenging discussions with my friends and colleagues, taught freshman college kids the basics of Western Civilization... What was I doing here?

I waited until Mancietti was out of breath.

"I understand why you are upset. You have every reason. Do you want us to talk about a solution?" I asked.

"There is no solution. You killed my life's work. You killed my children..."

And on, and on, and on he went through another fit of rage.

Finally, after over an hour of ranting, we started a two-way conversation. I told him that I had replacement yarn produced and ready for shipment at our factory. It could be here in twelve hours.

He looked at me incredulously. "What are you waiting for?" He asked. "You are killing me."

I registered immediately that he was not ready to drop us. That had been my hope. It was not that easy to change yarns in the weaving business. Lots of dye samples have to be made, and machines have to be adjusted and tested to achieve the same stretch and properties for the intended fabric. Mancietti had used our yarn for a long time. He did not want to switch.

"We need to settle some issues," I replied. "You have a huge claim against us..."

"You bet," he interrupted. "You owe me $480,000 by tomorrow morning. I will take Manson to the cleaners. He has it coming, that arrogant little ... "

I stopped him.

"Look, Mr. Mancietti, we are wasting time. I want to solve this for you. I want to solve this now. I want your factory to run again. I want your wife and your children to be happy. I want you to be happy."

I opened my hands to show that I had no weapons.

He calmed down.

We haggled for two hours. I got him to sign a delivery agreement for twenty-four months, with the caveat that we would not have any more quality problems. Otherwise, the contract was null and Mancietti would go to the competition. I thought that was fair. I also got him to reduce his claim. We agreed that the trucks would deliver the replacement yarn the next day. That would put him back into production within twenty-four hours.

Of course, we agreed that the replacement yarn was free of charge. I also offered to pay for setting up the new warps, estimated to be $24,000. In addition, I offered to pay him another $24,000 for lost profit, and $12,000 for lost wages. He agreed.

I had reduced the claim from $600,000, if we counted the time to get production back up and running, to $60,000. That was ten percent of the claim. Manson had said to minimize the claim. I delivered! When we shook hands that afternoon, Mancietti invited me to dinner to celebrate. After all that… Italians, you have to love them! Of course, I declined politely. I had to fly back and get his trucks on the road.

I was proud. Immensely proud. When I got back to England that night, I thought about how Manson was going to be impressed, and how the Vice President of the European operation was going to notice me.

The next morning, I came into the office at 7:00 AM. I wanted to send those trucks on the road as soon as possible. Manson was in his office. I popped my head in.

"How did it go?" he asked.

I smiled and let the delivery agreement sail onto his desk.

"He will keep buying from us," I said, "and I minimized the claim."

Manson looked happy.

"We will end up paying $60,000," I added self-assuredly.

"$60,000?" Manson huffed. "Are you nuts? I asked you to make this claim go away. I am not paying for it."

Go away, I thought. He never said that. He said "minimize." He knew we had to pay something.

"Call him back, tell him no yarn unless he drops the claim." Manson waved me away. I could not believe my ears. All this work, all this abuse, and now this? I had faced Mancietti, who had a valid grievance, with my boss's promise to support me in finding a solution to retain the customer and minimize the claim. I put my reputation on the line to get this outcome against overwhelming odds. I made the decision to stick to my guns.

"Marmaduke, I am not doing it," I said. "He will drop us like a hot potato. If you want to call him, he is your baby!" I pointed at his phone.

"Fine," Manson said dismissively, "I'll call him."

He did. We lost the customer. We also lost ten more weavers because they heard about the problem and did not want to take the risk. I was devastated. What had gone wrong? I left the company less than two years later. Manson's bigotry and selfishness had taken its toll on me.

The lesson of this case is this: Never pursue a goal that is not measurable! When Manson said minimize, I took ten percent to be a great success. He wanted to pay nothing. This was a good lesson to learn. I never again went into a negotiation without SMART goals.

Key Concepts and Factors that Impacted the Outcome of this Case:

- Pressure strategy and tactics
- Body language
- Goal-setting

CASE #4

I got to know a great logistics company during one of my previous jobs. The container line owned its own ships, called on few, small and accessible ports, and had excellent access to trucking companies picking up and delivering containers. As a supplier of batteries to BMW, I used this company exclusively. This container line provided excellent results for high-risk and just-in-time deliveries, spanning two continents.

When I started my own business importing German-made windows and doors to the United States, I naturally called on this supplier to provide the logistics for me. I had worked with the supplier for many years and had had good experiences. I also personally knew the senior management well. Most importantly, I remembered the price structure that we had for the BMW business, a much larger shipping volume than what my company could provide. The shipping line granted me my old prices and we worked well together for five years.

However, things changed around 2006. The dollar exchange rate turned against us in a detrimental way, adding forty percent to our purchasing cost for the windows. Oil prices also increased significantly at the same time, adding to the raw material cost of our products, as well as to transportation costs. We felt squeezed from multiple sides. After exhausting all partnership tactics with the container line to help me cut cost, I started to look at the competition. I knew that my supplier was not the cheapest, and I accepted that additional cost as the price for punctuality and the great service we received. However, over the previous five years I really had not checked the market. Now, when I did, I was shocked. I received quotes that were thirty percent below my current prices with the container line.

I decided to change my approach, and confronted my supplier directly with the much lower competitor prices. I received a snub. Clearly, my supplier was not dependent on my business. Much larger customers, mostly in the tobacco industry, provided their main revenue. The senior executive, whom I had known for a decade, basically told me that if I thought I could get a better deal elsewhere, I should do it. He could not help me. After a particularly confrontational phone call, we even hung up on each other.

The regional sales manager working under him called afterwards and begged me not to leave. He had no authority to offer a discount. Young and fairly inexperienced, he had taken over this region only three months earlier. He told me that one of the big accounts in that region had been a large tobacco company. As he begged me to reconsider, I learned that his company had a huge imbalance of containers. Way more containers left the US than were coming to the US from Europe. He really needed our freight! Without a discount, I told him, I could not afford his company. He said he had no authority. Since his boss already told me to get lost, I switched suppliers that day.

We switched our next two orders to the new supplier; four containers next week, and another two the week after. Our logistics staff did not like the new company. It was a much larger container line with huge ships that called on many ports on each voyage. The interaction with the booking department and customer service was impersonal and cold. Our old supplier's staff had grown to be like extended family to us. A disaster was brewing.

Shipping the two containers scheduled for the second week with the new supplier turned into a nightmare. The container company did something that had not happened to me in twenty years, and it was for the same the reason I had worked with the small container line in the first place: Our containers were bumped.

Typically, what happens is that a container stays at the pier for the next ship when space is overbooked, or a much more important customer makes an emergency request. Our old container line never once bumped us. But this case was even worse. The new supplier unloaded two of our containers in Cape Town, South Africa, and simply left them there. The customer service people could neither tell us where the containers were, nor how to access them, let alone when they would be shipped to us. I spent several nights on the phone trying to find anyone with knowledge and the ability to do something. Not receiving our delivery on time meant that we had to delay the installation of the windows and doors at a large, ten-million-dollar project. We could be fined for delaying the project in the worst case. In the best case, we would never get an order from this customer again, costing us millions in revenue.

The large container line that we had contracted with remained completely unresponsive. After much haggling, threats of legal action, and several sleepless nights, the two containers in Cape Town finally made it onto another ship from a different shipping line. I had found a freight brokerage company that was willing and able to switch the transportation companies. I paid double the original amount for these shipments, but at least I got them back on the ocean. However, when they arrived in port in Charleston, SC, Customs impounded the shipment. Switching transportation companies halfway raised all kinds of red flags. We now had to pay for customs agents to take our containers apart and search them. Plus, it was another week lost!

We had forecasted a solid volume of two containers per week sailing from Germany. I certainly did not want to have any more nightmares such as this. My expected savings with the new shipper had turned into higher costs and worse, created an upset customer. I had the choice of calling back my old supplier only three weeks after having left. Or, I could keep saving on the deliveries and somehow improve the situation with my new supplier. After looking at all my options, I determined that the latter was not really a choice. I had to get my old shipping company back. Now, I was in a total time crunch. The next containers were ready to load this same week. But how could I get the supplier back? I hoped I could come back, but I knew it wouldn't be at a discount. I expected another price increase.

I had two strategic options: Call my senior contact at the old supplier, grovel, ask for help, and place the order. There was a small chance, based on our long-term relationship that I would get to keep my old price. More likely was the chance that I would have to accept a price increase. Or, as a second option, find a way to pressure the old supplier into taking me back at a discount. I had little leverage for that strategy, I had time constraints, and I had no viable alternative. I could not easily hide that fact when calling just three weeks after leaving.

Take a minute and think about this case. What would you have done?

On Rare Occasions Bullying Works! Or does it?
Here is the rest of the story:

Call me crazy, but I decided to use a pressure strategy. I know, rule number one: Never use pressure if you are in a weak bargaining position. In this case, I neither had leverage nor an alternative. I took a calculated gamble. I banked on the other side did not knowing my situation with the new supplier. My old supplier could assume that I had a problem, but without anyone in my company leaking such information, they could not be sure. No one was leaking, I could enforce that.

What was my goal? Objectively, the worst case was that I had to stay with the new supplier. I did not consider that a possibility because I was confident my old supplier would take me back. I knew that they had a container imbalance in my region. Every freight order counted. That is why I was reasonably sure they would take me back. I just didn't know at what price.

I remembered how desperately the salesman had tried to retain me as a customer. I decided to plan for two separate strategies: First, I would call the young salesman and use pressure; and, if that did not work, I would call the senior sales executive, his boss, grovel, and ask for help.

"John (the regional sales rep), this is Harry with Henselstone Window and Door Systems. How are you?" I initiated the conversation on the phone.

"Hi Harry, great to hear from you. How are things? Are you happy with your new shipper?" Wise guy.

"You know, I am really pissed at you guys. This new company is not the same. They are way cheaper, but their customer service is no good. My staff hates to talk to their people in some type of call center in who-knows-where. Every day I hear, 'I wished I could talk to Suzie (the customer service rep in Hamburg).' I just don't know why you guys are so bull-headed." I sounded angry and frustrated.

"Well, we miss you, too. I don't know what to do, though," he opened up. "Do you have a problem?"

"No, I don't have a problem. I am saving thirty percent on my freight. Doesn't sound like a problem to me," I retorted, "but I am not happy. My people asked me to give you all one last chance. To get them off my back, here it is..."

I continued: "This is what I want you to do: You call George (Senior VP of Sales), whom I have known since he used diapers, and give him this message from me: Here is one last chance. I will pay a premium for your service, but I cannot work with your current pricing. I have two container orders sitting right here on my desk. Tomorrow at 8:00 AM I am sending them off. If you give me a decent number, you get those. If you give me a great number, I will give you an exclusive contract for three years. It's totally up to George. Let me know."

I hung up. Let's see what the sales rep could do for me.

Sometimes you are just lucky, or the other side is too tired to win, not prepared, worn down, or, who knows? Two hours after our phone call, John, the sales rep called me.

"We have a number. It might not be what you are looking for, but George wants you to consider it."

"Shoot," I said. He threw out a bunch of container fees, call ports, delivery ports, inland freight, BAF charges...

"Hold it, John," I stopped him. "Make this quick and easy. I don't have time to go through all your numbers and figure out if this is a good deal or not. What percentage do I save on my bottom line?"

There was silence on the line.

"John, are you there?" I tapped the phone. "Hellooo."

"Yes, yes," came the reply. Now he seemed to be stuttering. Either I made him nervous, and he had slipped into the micro level, or his offer was bad.

"John, you seem nervous. Please, don't waste my time. What is the number?" I pressed. I heard whispering in the background. It sounded like George was sitting with him. Interesting!

"I am not nervous; I am scrambling a bit. We can save you five percent," John finally said.

On cue, I immediately blurted out, "Not enough, John. I am saving thirty percent right now."

I heard more whispering in the background. If George was engaged, he must be interested, I thought. He wanted me back. I had already reached my goal, but this was too much fun to quit just yet.

"Harry," George's voice came on the phone.

"Oh, hey George, what are you doing here? Am I too rough on John?" I laughed.

He did not flinch. "Harry, are you giving us exclusivity?" George asked.

"Exclusivity?" I paused.

George reiterated, "Yes, exclusivity."

I let him simmer.

"I really need something from you to make a deal," George pushed.

"You need 'something'?" I toyed with him.

"That's right. Three years?" George asked.

I felt a deal coming together.

"Fine." I tried to hide my anxiety. He had something up his sleeve.

"Can we limit the delivery locations to South Carolina and New York?" George asked. These two states covered eighty percent of our sales.

"No," I said. "Why would we limit the locations? We are selling anywhere, George, Florida, Tennessee. What are you saying?"

George sighed.

"Okay, you get the old prices for all locations. But I will cut you a deal for a special 10% discount on your two main delivery regions if you give us all your business for three years. What do you think?"

I decided that it was time for the bow. This was a great deal. I had achieved a significant discount, probably eight percent across the board. I had solved my immediate shipping crisis. And my service level forecast with customers just switched to sunshine.

"George," I answered, "you made my life hell for months now. But for some reason, I still love you. We have a deal. Give John a hug from me, too. He's a good man!"

To this day, fifteen years later, we use the same shipping line—exclusively. We've had a few price negotiations since then, but neither I nor my supplier ever took our business to the brink again. George and I remained good friends. I called him and wished him all the best when he retired a few years ago. I told him how much I appreciated him helping out our company over the years, especially in times of hardship. I never disclosed how deep the morass was that I had maneuvered my company into when we clashed that one time in all the years of working together. I am sure now that he knew all along. He helped me out because he wanted to. That means if initially I would have asked for his help, groveled, and given him a long-term agreement, he might have given me the same deal. I could have avoided all the trouble of switching companies.

Key Concepts and Factor that Helped Win this Case:
- Starting position, calculating risk
- Pressure strategy and tactics
- Goal-setting
- Negotiating over the phone

About the Author

Heribert von Feilitzsch, MA, MBA, has spent the past 30 years working in the textile, automotive, construction, and consulting industries as an industrial engineer, salesman, market development manager, and executive. During the 1990s, von Feilitzsch managed a joint venture in the automotive industry between two fierce competitors that taught him to hone his negotiation skills.

He learned to be highly sensitized to reading other people, their cultures, professional backgrounds, motivations, mind-sets, and goals. Von Feilitzsch started his own company in 2001 in the international trade and construction industries. He still runs his small, but successful company with little purchasing power after nearly twenty years. He also stayed connected with corporate customers from his previous career while expanding his company. The author has worked for the past fifteen years, in parallel to running his own business, as a negotiation trainer, coach, and ghost negotiator for large international corporations in the automotive, energy generation, and medical industries in Europe, Asia, and North America. His customers include Daimler Corporation, Volkswagen Group, Volvo Cars, Volvo Group, and Siemens. He is the author of four books and numerous peer-reviewed articles.

Acknowledgments

Many people have helped me conceive of this project. First and foremost, my friend Frieder Gamm helped me understand what I was doing and why it worked. We have known each other for twenty-five years, negotiated against each other, and worked together on important projects. I have worked for the Frieder Gamm Group during the last fifteen years as a coach, trainer, lecturer, and the only detail-oriented person on the entire team! I want to thank the FGG team for helping us become true leaders in the training and professional negotiating arena together. I am grateful for the opportunity, and look forward to working together for decades to come.

My three boys sharpened my negotiation skills immensely, as I mentioned before. I am embarrassed to admit that I have lost quite a few negotiations over the years to them. They had prepared better and executed to perfection. I love you all! My son Matthias, in particular, offered to model for the body language session. He assisted me for a year in the seminars I gave and knows all of the material in this book. He spent years honing his strategic, communicative, and psychological negotiation skills. The biggest advantage Matthias has is his youth.

Counterparts in tough negotiations consistently underestimate him. That is the deadliest weapon in his arsenal.

Mina von Feilitzsch, my talented daughter-in-law, produced the majority of photographs in this book. An internationally successful professional photographer in her own right, she has a keen eye for the perfect shot. Thank you for taking the time and for making the photography for this book so stunning.

My wife has been my partner for almost three decades. While definitely being the Farmer type, she somehow copes with my ever-changing, ever-exploring, ever-evolving professional life and continues to stand by me. I know how hard it is. Thank you!

I could not have done this without the help of Rosa DeBerry King, a fantastic editor, designer, and author in her own right. She made this text flow, designed the layout, and kept my feet to the ground! Thank you.

Fred Opitz and his team at Machwerk in Ludwigburg, Germany have supported my work creatively for over two decades. We worked together on incredibly creative book covers, websites, and even a film project. Thank you for your creative spirit and long years of friendship, and, yes, another great book cover.

Ute Gamm conceived of the brilliance of making psychological and behavioral science concepts digestible for the professional negotiator. Her experience in early childhood education and pedagogy created the method for making complicated concepts accessible to students of negotiating.

Many thanks to my friend of over forty years, Hannes Gebhardt. As a psychologist, he was gentle and sensitive in his criticism and feedback. Thanks to him, my venturing into psychology and behavioral sciences is thoroughly rooted in science despite the simplifications I had to inflict on it during the course of writing this book. He deserves full credit for the development of S.M.A.R.T.[+] as a psychological dimension to the Doran model.

Finally, I am grateful to everyone who traveled with me on my professional journey throughout the years. I am grateful to all my former bosses, including the ones that taught me how not to manage. I always try to learn from everyone, and I am grateful for the lessons I have received. I also want to express my gratitude to the professors in the Wake Forest University Babcock School of Business. Going through the executive MBA program at that school changed my life. Thank you!

Further Reading

Berne, Eric, *Intuition and Ego States*. New York: Harper and Row Publisher, 1977

Fisher, Roger, and Danny Ertel, *Getting Ready to Negotiate: A Step-by-Step Guide to Preparing for any Negotiation*. New York: Penguin-Random House, 1995

Fisher, Roger, and Daniel Shapiro, *Beyond Reason: Using Emotions as You Negotiate*. London: Penguin Group, 2005

Fisher, Roger, William Ury, and Bruce Patton, *Getting to Yes: Negotiating agreement without giving in*. London: Penguin Group, 1981

Garrett, Gregory A., *Contract Negotiations: Skills, Tools, and Best Practices*. Chicago: CCH Incorporated, 2005

Gates, Steve, *The Negotiation Book: Definitive Guide to Successful Negotiating*. Chichester: John Wiley and Sons Ltd., 2011

Kahneman, Daniel, *Thinking Fast and Slow*. 7th edition. Toronto: Doubleday Canada, 2011

Leyshon, Aaron, *Negotiate without Negotiating: An Introvert's Guide to Getting More and Stressing Less.* Unknown: A Million Doubts, 2018

Mehrabian, Albert, *Nonverbal Communication.* New York: Transaction Publishers, 1972

Navarro, Joe, *What Every Body is Saying: An Ex-FBI Agent's Guide to Speed-Reading People.* New York: Harper Collins Publishers, 2008

Noesner, Gary, *Stalling for Time: My Life as an FBI Hostage Negotiator.* New York: Random House, 2010

O'Brien, Jonathan, *Negotiation for Procurement and Supply Chain Professionals.* 2nd edition. New York: Kogan-Page Company, 2016

Shell, Richard G., *Bargaining for Advantage: Negotiation Strategies for Reasonable People.* New York: Penguin- Random House, 1999

Sun Tzu, *The Art of War.* China: 5th Century BC
Ury, William, *Getting Past No: Negotiating in Difficult Situations.* New York: Bantam Books, 1993

Voss, Chris, Raz Tahl, *Never Split the Difference – Negotiating as if your life depended on it.* New York: Harper Business Publishing, 2016